Adventures
— *in* —
Simple Living

Adventures
—— in ——
Simple Living

A
CREATION-CENTERED
SPIRITUALITY

Rich Heffern

CROSSROAD · NEW YORK

✪ Printed on recycled paper

1994

The Crossroad Publishing Company
370 Lexington Avenue, New York, NY 10017

Printed in the United States of America

Library of Congress Cataloging-in-Publication Data

Heffern, Rich.
    Adventures in simple living : a creation-centered spirituality /
Rich Heffern.
       p. cm.
    Includes bibliographical references.
    ISBN 0-8245-1400-9
    1. Simplicity—Religious aspects. 2. Life style. 3. Spiritual
life. I. Title.
BJ1496.H44 1944
248.4–dc20
                                       93-45875
                                           CIP

Contents

Introduction

C AN WE LEAD OUR LIVES in ways that are satisfying and richly fulfilling while also just and
environmentally benign, so that everyone in
the world can live in similar ways without damaging
the earth? This question is fast becoming the central
one of our time.

What is enough? Over the last few decades finding a satisfactory answer to this query has suddenly
taken on an immense urgency. Besides the distress-
ing mega-threats to the environment, widespread
poverty and hunger plague the world's human population. We can blame Madison Avenue advertisers
or multinational corporations or governments and
politicians for the heedless injustices and run-amok
destruction of our beautiful planet in the name of
more consumer goods on display at the local mall. But
who buys and uses the products? Who is responsible?
Where does the buck stop? If we all do fifty simple
things to save the planet, will that be enough? Can

we restore generosity to our human economy and curb its ravenous appetite for resources? How can we turn things around and give back to our world its lost heart and soul? How can we achieve security and sufficiency in our lives, stopping short of inequity, waste, and clutter?

Many have found that one good means to that end is to live in much simpler ways — a personal response to the need for more just and ecological lifestyles. This book is about that kind of simple living. It is not the final word on the subject or the definitive discussion — just one person's exploration, a half dozen hikes up to some hilly ground to take a look around and get the lay of the land. On these hikes I use the following terms almost interchangeably: "simple living," "living lightly and generously," and "the ways of simple living." By these words I mean the daily choices, strategies, prioritizing, and wider decisions one makes in the attempt to live moderately and to flourish without a lot of money and dependent largely upon unmarketable pleasures and satisfactions, with full hearts and without a lot of clutter and stuff in our attics and garages.

The degree of influence an active and energetic commitment to simple living has on our everyday choices and on the larger decisions of life will vary according to the level of seriousness and the fluid, ever-changing situations and responsibilities in which we find ourselves. There is a wide spectrum of behaviors that might fall under the heading of simple living. There is an even wider variety of reasons people make these choices and attempt these strategies and disciplines in their living.

There are probably hundreds of thousands now who make some deliberate effort to live simply. Myra and John live in the northern suburbs of Chicago and put plastic bins in their garage for recyclables. They spend a few minutes each day separating and sorting and then an hour a month taking the bins to drop-off centers. Both also choose to ride the public transit to their jobs every weekday rather than driving. When they recently bought a new car, they opted for one without air conditioning or other added features. They are busy raising their two children. The whole family attempts to eat a bit lower on the food chain than is widely done, limiting their consumption of meat. They also limit the amount of time they spend watching television, choosing to read to and talk with their children most evenings.

In rural New Mexico, Cyril and Ed card the wool and spin yarn from a dozen sheep they raise in their four-acre backyard. They also keep goats for milk and make their own cheese when they have time. Both are self-employed computer programmers and work as consultants out of their home, a sprawling adobe structure they built themselves. When they must travel to faraway cities for conferences or vacations, they take the train rather than drive.

Marie is an accountant who lives in Kansas City. She lives alone in an elegant apartment on the south side for which she pays a modest rent. Marie spends a good deal of her spare time exploring her inner life —

through journaling, keeping track of her dreams, spiritual reading, and long talks with her friends. What's left of her time is spent in vigorous volunteer work, helping maintain a women's spirituality center and keeping the financial records for a small alternative newspaper.

In southeastern Kansas, Eleanor and Robert alternate between living a year or two in their small-town community with a year or two in ministry. Eleanor works as an administrator in a local college, while Robert serves as minister in the local Mennonite church. A year ago they finished a two-year stint as teachers in the Navajo lands of northern Arizona. They buy their clothes in local thrift shops. Robert bicycles every day to his church office.

In Portland, Oregon, Marcus and Linda are forty-somethings who love above all travel and adventure. They work for several years (he as a teacher and she as a nurse) until they've earned enough money to coast for a while and then quit their jobs to spend six or eight months traveling the world. In 1991 they toured Indonesia, Malaysia, and Burma. My wife and I got cards they sent postmarked from Rangoon and Singapore. The mid-1980s found them living for a year in Costa Rica. In a year or two they plan to spend a season or two in Africa.

Vickie deliberately chooses not to have an income level high enough to require her to pay federal taxes, because 50 to 60 percent goes to pay for war — past, present, and future. She earns some money painting houses and doing substitute teaching. She spends her time working as a community organizer and re-furbishing her old three-story house in the inner city.

Beth and Mary subsist almost entirely on organi-cally grown vegetables, poultry, and cheese, which they purchase in bulk quantities from a cooperative food-buying club. They live in a roomy dome-shaped house standing on bottomland Mary inherited twenty years ago in the Missouri Ozarks. They make their liv-ing weaving rope sandals and hammocks and selling these goods at crafts fairs. Both also play hand-made musical instruments in a local bluegrass band.

Generosity and responsibility have taken root in these people's lives. The need to celebrate and en-joy the world's best gifts has a high priority. Some commit themselves for overtly religious or spiritual reasons. Others make the attempt out of concern for the environment or compassion for the other life with which we share the planet. Still others swim against the tide of our culture and society because they just can't abide employment in a full-time job or working for someone else or the stressful rigors and heartless oppressions of the system. Many just want to free up lots of time, to live in an uncluttered way, in order to devote themselves to their enthusiasms and loves.

Most can probably explain forthrightly their mo-tivation for undertaking these endeavors of simple living — and these reasons will vary as widely as do the life experiences, personalities, philosophies, pol-itics, and creativity of the people themselves. In fact, a book of in-depth interviews with a dozen people around the country who attempt to live simply would be a very interesting one to read.

Whatever the explicit reasons for practicing simple living, the daily choices, prioritizing, and wider decisions that must be made – the conscious "lifestyle" involved – embody, I believe, a practical description of some spiritual condition, ranging from a high value put on independence and self-reliance through a deep-seated concern for the impact our living makes on the planet, all the way to being convinced that the slightest compromise with our techno-consumer society is cooperation with evil and to be avoided at all costs. The consciously simple lifestyle is an outward reflection of some developed and developing inner reality.

Over 150 years ago America's most famous pursuer of simple living, Henry David Thoreau, articulated in *Walden* his reasons for living in a one-room cabin built by himself in the woods near a pond: to savor life, to suck the marrow from its bones, to live deliberately and sturdily. "I am convinced," he wrote, "that to maintain oneself on this earth is not a hardship, but a pastime, if we will live simply and wisely." One critic called his work the most original in American literature. His timeless classic describes at length a spirituality of simple living.

Because of my own background, history, quirks, idiosyncrasies, strengths, shortcomings, and inclinations, my experience of simple living has always meshed the daily choices and larger decisions together with what is nowadays called a "creation-centered" spirituality. The "lifestyle" I practice is driven by, intertwines with, and is both informed and inspired by that spirituality. The pages that follow explore a spirituality of simple living. Marsha Sinetar, author of *Ordinary People as Monks and Mystics,* said, "Spirituality is an intelligence in its own right: useful, tactical and immensely creative." In our society this intelligence seems to be on the rise and taking a more active role in our living in many new and fascinating ways — as together we face the disruptions, threats, and upheavals of the last decade of the twentieth century and beyond.

No one person or group "does" simple living better than another. There is no guidebook to follow. Everyone who is so inclined starts from a particular location on a complicated and mysterious web, a place that is unique. There is ample room in this enterprise of simple living for self-righteousness and snobbishness, opportunity to make molehills into mountains and mountains into molehills. More than twenty-five hundred years ago, the Buddha said, "Seeker, empty the boat, lighten the load, be free of craving and judgment and hatred, and feel the joy of the way." Still good advice, I have discovered that I must with all my heart renew the commitment to it every single day, sometimes many times a day.

Personally I own a pickup truck, a personal computer and printer, an expensive camera, and some other accouterments of the consumer wonder world.

Mine is not a very spartan lifestyle by many standards. Nevertheless I would not hesitate to number myself among the ranks of those making a serious stab at simple living. "Money or possessions or activities themselves do not corrupt simplicity," writes David Shi, author of *The Simple Life*, "but the love of money, the craving for possessions, and the prison of activities do." The will is there to constantly strive to be free of these cravings. Each day I renew the struggle in any number of ways – and experience small triumphs and many stumblings. Every day I find myself wrestling with one or another aspect of the ongoing dilemma and challenge of attempting to live consciously, responsibly, and with moderation in these last decades of the twentieth century. I believe I am describing with my daily living the spirituality Marsha Sinetar writes about – that active, searching, tactical intelligence that is every single day challenged in a host of ways to be creative and wise and useful.

It is not simple to live simply. It takes energy and skill. Conflict and tension between many opposing factors must be steadily and uncomplainingly borne and creatively confronted. At times it feels like a hugely complex chess game in which one weighs and balances the consequences of an array of moves or choices against the background of countermoves, trying to achieve the position on the board that best honors both our commitment to simple living and all of our other responsibilities. Often it's a matter of making trade-offs or truces, plea-bargaining, or just deciding in which battles we can adequately fight and prevail and in which it might be wiser to retreat or surrender.

What's more, in all kinds of ways our consumer society mounts hurdles and roadblocks in our path. A television comedienne talks of visiting the mall to buy a wastebasket for her new apartment. The clerk put her wastebasket into a sack. She carried the sack home and then threw it into the wastebasket she had just bought. "Get real!" she yelped and threw up her hands.

Hers is an apt parable for what we're up against. One really can't blame the clerk, the store — or anyone in particular. Such wasteful policies and practices are the result of countless incremental decisions and choices made thoughtlessly by all of us over a long period of time, the end results of which are fast destroying our planet's life support systems. The reversal of such destructive ways, if it happens, will no doubt result from countless incremental decisions and choices made thoughtfully over time. Individual efforts do finally add up.

Part of our job description as simple living people is to keep at this task. It's an important one. We must describe with our lives the future we want to see for our children. It may or may not be enough. The jury is out, and no one knows what the verdict will be.

One thing I do know: simple living is a great adventure. It seems as though for many of us it's the only adventure left in a world that has become marketable and expendable to a thoughtless hucksterism that spreads like cancer. It is an adventure like the late Edward Abbey describes in his blessing:

> May your trails be crooked, winding, lonesome, dangerous, leading to the most amazing view. May your mountains rise into and above the clouds. May your rivers flow without end, meandering through pastoral valleys tinkling with bells, past temples and castles and poets' towers into a dark primeval forest, through miasmal and mysterious swamps down into a desert of red rock, blue mesas, domes and pinnacles and grottos of endless stone, and down again into a deep vast ancient unknown chasm where bars of sunlight blaze on profiled cliffs, where deer walk across white sand beaches, where storms come and go as lightning clangs upon the high crags, where something strange and more beautiful and more full of wonder than your deepest dreams waits for you — beyond that next turning of the canyon walls.

Simple living is about praise and gratitude. Here I want to praise and express thanks to those who have generously helped me to live simply and (I hope) generously in turn, including my wife, Linda; to Bob and Sue in the Ozarks; to my parents who lived simply because it was necessary when they were young, but kept it up long before it was fashionable; to my lifelong friend, John Pocsik; to Rick and Judy Sleep; to Wally Kendrick; to Brothers Bill Kraus, Charles

Chaput, and Joseph McGlynn, Capuchins; to Virginia Woody; to Carol Meyer and Charles Lackamp; to my colleagues at National Catholic Reporter Publishing Company who put up with me, Art Winter and Carolyn Hoff; I'm grateful also to Michael Leach of Crossroad Publishing for his encouragement.

Chapter 1

The Adventure
of Simple Living

I T ALL STARTED in the blackberry patch. One hot
July day when I was a kid growing up in Kansas
City I was taken to an overgrown pasture outside of town where gallons of this delicious wild fruit
hung, free for the taking, on thorn-bristling vines that
drooped heavily toward the earth. We filled our pails
with berries until our hands were stained dark blue
and then hauled them home to use in pies, cobblers,
and homemade ice cream.

I can remember being spellbound beyond all reason, delighted and pleased that the local countryside
had provided all this bounteous harvest without any
sowing or cultivation on our part, but just by means
of its unheeded daily comings and goings: the spring
rains had fallen, the June sunshine had happened.

On those long July afternoons the fruit had ripened while the meadowlarks sang and the bluebirds warbled.

I have never forgotten the lesson of those pastures, long since gone to shopping malls. The earth takes care of us. She provides a pantry from which we draw our daily sustenance.

The flame of enthusiasm for simple living, I'm sure, was struck from such childhood experiences. It was fanned to life by other happenings. I remember when my mother bequeathed to me a venerable old Dutch oven that had been in the family for several generations. Cooking soup in a sturdy vessel that my grandmother had used and her mother before her provided rich satisfactions that all the expensive cookware in the best department stores couldn't duplicate. On a trip through the Southwest as a teenager, I can remember an afternoon when I spotted the jewelry-bedecked and colorfully dressed Navajo sheepherders and their simple dwellings made of native wood and stone, at home amid the dazzling splendor of that redrock country. Again, a spellbinding fascination and a beckoning call.

The first time a teacher in my Catholic grade school told us about Francis of Assisi, I rang like a bell. I understood the passion of this medieval man for simplicity, his urge to cultivate an intimacy with all of creation by limiting his wants and satisfying his needs in simple ways. Later in life, reading books by and about such other simple livers as Henry David

Thoreau, Dorothy Day, Gandhi, or Thomas Merton added to my understanding and heartened me to take further plunges.

Gifts from the Dark

Recently my wife and I spent a weekend in our little house way back in the woods in the Ozark mountains. We were miles from any town, hundreds from the nearest big city. Evening fell. There was no moon that night. In the country, a moonless night means a kind of enveloping darkness that we city-dwellers seldom experience any longer. My wife went to play cards with the neighbors for the evening and took the flashlight with her to light the way down the woodland path to the country road. I told her I'd be along later. When it was time for me to make my way through the woods I realized she had taken the only flashlight. Searching for some other light source, I found an old kerosene lamp. With the soot-blackened chimney sheltering the flickering flame, I made my way slowly along the twistings and turnings of the path, flanked on both sides by tall, fragrant pines. About halfway down the path, a night breeze came up suddenly and blew out my little lamp. Instantly the darkness swallowed me up. I stopped and stood there, thinking at that moment how much I would give for a single wooden match with which to relight my flame. But technology had I none. I stood with the useless lamp in my hand, stumped and more than a little afraid of the darkness – and gradually began to come alive.

As my eyes got used to the dark, I discovered that I could see, somewhat dimly, the silhouettes of the trees against the overcast skies. Far off, I could hear the lonely cry of an owl and the barking of a distant dog; nearer, the soft meditative dripping of raindrops left over from an early evening storm. The wonderful smells of the woodland, the aromas of damp leaf mold and pine needles, filled the air with a heady incense.

Slowly I began to feel my way long the path. My hands brushed against the rough, lichen-covered tree bark. My feet cautiously groped among the gnarled tree roots along the path. There was the ruffle and flap of feathered wings when I startled a sleeping bird out of a cedar sapling. I looked up. The clouds overhead were beginning to part. I could see patches of stars here and there. Some of them were down among the trees, looking like fugitives from the night sky, brilliant twinklings in among the dark branches. The pine trees were mute presences. The silence had a life all its own. Mystery was all around me.

Inside of me I felt a kind of thrill, a tingling, a delightful sense of expectation. It seemed that anything might happen, that adventures and revelations were just around the next bend in the path. I could feel the blood's flood pounding through my veins. At the same time, I was conscious of being filled with a sense of gentle love and affection for all of creation, especially its living things. I was sorry I'd disturbed the sleeping bird.

I never would have experienced the fullness and richness of that ordinary moment in the woods if my flame had not been blown out by an errant wind. I am not recommending we all go back to kerosene lamps and sod or log houses; I'm only suggesting that there is a dynamics to simplicity that has a lot to do with living life to the fullest and deepest extent. Later it came to me while reflecting on that woodland encounter with the night that there are two very valuable spiritual gifts that simplicity gives to us. It seems that the more we can strip our lives down to essentials, the more deliberately and awake we can live, with few wants and more time for silence and contemplation, the more we have access to these resources. The more lightly we walk on this earth the more she gives to us.

I call these spiritual gifts *inner smiling* and *outgoingness of heart.*

Inner smiling is that glad, happy, energized, and fulfilled feeling that comes when one is in touch with one's own heart's desire and with the honesty and sanity of genuine things. Inner smiling comes to us when we are in the midst of the natural world or when we are exercising our own creativity and resourcefulness. It comes to us when we are engaged in meaningful and productive work. Inner smiling is the natural state of the artist, the mystic, the stargazer, the good parent, the gardener, the holy person, the farmer, the craftsperson, the backpacker, the child — of anyone who is wholeheartedly centered in a worthy task or in healthy play.

Outgoingness of heart, on the other hand, is that feeling of intimacy with and compassion for all of life. "There are tears in things," wrote the poet Virgil two thousand years ago, "and all things doomed to die touch the heart." Outgoingness of heart surely drove Francis of Assisi to give up his heritage of wealth and write his canticle of praise to Brother Sun and Sister Moon. What else could have lured Mother Teresa to the slums of Calcutta? Jesus taught his followers that there were only two great commandments. Both of his imperatives require outgoingness of heart. And an ancient Tibetan Buddhist saying goes: "The experience of emptiness engenders compassion."

Both inner smiling and outgoingness of heart are essential equipment for anyone cultivating a spirituality; they are prerequisites for discipleship. These spiritual dividends, it seems, are more likely to be paid out to us when we are involved in simple, unwasteful pursuits. They are perhaps more easily found while pedaling a bicycle, for example, than while driving a car; on a train rather than in a speeding jet; while reading a good book rather than while watching TV. Walking, the simplest means of getting around there is, is one of the best single ways to reap a quick and bountiful harvest.

Harvest from Emptiness

Father Richard Rohr, founder of the Center for Action and Contemplation and the New Jerusalem Community, likes to call it "emptiness," this way of cultivating a healthy poverty and simplicity in our lives. And the importance of emptiness is that it is essential to becoming *who we really are*. When we become too busy, too caught up in the fast currents of modern living (especially with its unbridled consumerism), too dependent on the tube to entertain us and an array of conveniences to save us time (which then must be spent working to pay for the conveniences), then we cheat ourselves outrageously out of the time, the peace, and the silence needed to cultivate ourselves as unique persons.

Both inner smiling and outgoingness of heart, I'm convinced, are byproducts of being centered within and closely intimate with who we really are, what the monk and writer Thomas Merton calls "our true self." And only in emptying ourselves and in unhurried quiet can we really get to know and make friends with our wondrously crafted inner landscape, with the rich and colorful weave of strengths and frailties, passions and sadnesses, urges, compulsions, and poignant absurdities, foibles, dreams, and generosities, all happening at the same time, that make us a unique, one-of-a-kind patchwork and an indispensable part of the divine plan. "The glory of God," wrote Irenaeus in the third century, "is a human fully alive." In simplicity and in self-emptying we can, paradoxically, have life to the full.

The real secret is that voluntary poverty and simplicity can be fun. A commitment to live in simple, unwasteful ways challenges us to limit our wants and to satisfy our needs through our own resourcefulness, ingenuity, and hard, but satisfying, work. We must dig deep, all the way down to that restless longing and yearning for the exercise of our creativity that prowls, mostly unsatisfied, within us.

Searching through thrift shops, learning to cook or bake bread from scratch, taking the bus to work, riding bicycles, planting and caring for a garden, volunteering at the local soup kitchen or recycling center, mending clothes and repairing things ourselves — all of these activities are endless sources of entertainment and deep emotional satisfaction. They require of us humility, faith, forbearance, generosity, and (above all) imagination. In return, there is a kind of boldness, good humor, heartiness, and gratitude for life that accompany embarking upon this particular adventure.

Recently I took some extra time and returned from a conference 600 miles away by taking the train home instead of an airline flight. The rail route followed the course of the Missouri River for some 150 miles outside of St. Louis, and I sat back in the comfortable seat and watched the shifting afternoon light on the river. Now and then I would catch a glimpse of a great blue heron gracefully taking off through the cottonwoods or a wintering bald eagle cruising magnificently along the river bank. As the train passed through the little river towns, the chief conductor (who apparently was a history buff) announced the stops over the intercom and then recounted some fascinating stories and lore about Jesse James and other outlaws, marauders, and scalawags who had haunted these parts in the bloody Civil War days.

After darkness had fallen, a troop of giggling girl scouts came aboard on their way home from a field trip to the state capitol. When their tickets had been punched and they had settled down in their seats, one of the conductors came back to our car and planted himself in the aisle. He reached into the pockets of his uniform jacket and pulled out a worn deck of cards and some pieces of rope. He then proceeded to perform magic and card tricks for the girls.

As the miles rolled by to the tune of the rails' clickety-clack and the mournful wail of the locomotive's horn, the conductor, his ruddy face creased with smile wrinkles, kept up a running patter of silly jokes as he bedazzled the girls with his legerdemain and sleight-of-hand. He pulled silver dollars out of ears. Silk scarves vanished into thin air. Pieces of rope mysteriously reknitted themselves together. The Ace of Spades turned up in the most unlikely places. The girls were completely enchanted.

And the rest of us in the car, too, seemed full to the brim with good feelings of community. Stranger visited with stranger, pausing now and then to look up for an "ooh" or an "aah." One fellow went off to the lounge car and returned with a round of hot chocolate for all. Another took photos and then collected names and addresses, promising to send copies to each of us. Everyone was under the spell of that magical Amtrak employee whose inner smiling and outgoingness of heart had spilled over contagiously until we were all smitten.

I know I would have missed all these riches if I had flown the friendly skies.

Simple living, it seems, is one of two ways to achieve great wealth. Annie Dillard tells, in her Pulitzer Prize–winning book *Pilgrim at Tinker Creek*, that when she was a child she used to stash copper pennies along the sidewalks of her hometown. She just hid them away so that strangers would find them as they walked along. "It is dire poverty indeed," she wrote, "when a person is so malnourished they won't stoop to pick up a penny. But if you cultivate a healthy poverty and simplicity, then, since the world is in fact planted with pennies, you have with your poverty bought a lifetime of days. It is that simple."

Consider this adventure of simple living. In this day of both dwindling resources and environmental awareness, it is a way to help save the earth for future generations. And, as we have seen, it is a way to harness the energies of love. It is also a surer way to riches than the hope of winning a lottery ticket. It is that simple.

❀

Why try to live voluntarily in simple ways? Here are eight other good reasons according to the Center for

Science in the Public Interest, a research organization in Washington, D.C., that investigates public interest issues, including energy, environmental protection, consumer safety, and nutrition. They come from the Center's book, *Ninety Ways to a Simple Lifestyle*. Add them all up, pressed down and shaken together, and what you have is a kind of complete program for implementing a holistic spirituality into your life.

1. **Symbolic.** Simple living promotes solidarity with the world's poor and reduces the hypocrisy of our overconsumptive lifestyle. We live in a country whose people make up less than 5 percent of the world's population, yet we consume over 25 percent of the world's resources (according to the World-watch Institute).

2. **Ecological.** Voluntary simple living reduces our use of these natural resources, lessens pollution and waste, creates an awareness in ourselves and for others that we must live in harmony with the natural world. A recent ad recruiting members for an environmental organization featured a portrait of the skipper of the Exxon *Valdez*. The caption underneath read: "It wasn't his driving that caused the oil spill. It was *yours*." There is truth there. The planet cannot stand much more of our wasteful ways of living.

3. **Health.** Simple living lessens tensions and anxiety, encourages more rest and relaxation, reduces use of harmful chemicals (alcohol, drugs, pesticides, etc.), and helps create inner harmony. Medical experts estimate that 80 percent of all hospital ad-

missions in the nation nowadays are for stress-related illnesses! No doubt about it, living less frantically is good for you.

4. **Economic.** Simple living saves money, reduces the need to work long hours, and increases both number and quality of jobs.

5. **Human-oriented.** Voluntary simplicity provides greater opportunities to work together and to share resources with one's neighbors. Living simply can bring us closer together in sound communities, healthy families, and more livable neighborhoods.

6. **Nature-oriented.** Simple living helps us to appreciate the serenity and sanity of nature, its silence, its changes of season, and its creatures. A healthy appreciation of the natural world can satisfy some of those aches and yearnings for connection and for belonging that we try to medicate or anesthetize with drugs or submerge with consumerism.

7. **Social.** Simple living induces frustration with the limited scope of individual action and incites us to move to social- and political-action levels. We are more likely, for example, to participate in our city's neighborhood associations or issue-oriented groups or to volunteer for much-needed community service as a way to become involved in making our community a better place. Imagine the kind of society that would emerge if voluntary simplicity became the predominant lifestyle in our country.

8. **Spiritual.** As we have discussed, simple living allows more time for prayer and meditation, for inner smiling and outgoingness of heart.

Chapter 2

Live Kindly

WINTER'S DROWSE IS OVER. Spring is well advanced in its occupation. In late April I trudge slowly down an old logging road that runs the length of a wooded valley in the midwestern Ozark mountains. My boots are wet from the dew.

In air so fresh it's like filtered through lemons, the morning unfolds as I walk. Oak and hickory saplings ruffle in the slight breeze. Pale leaves are just emerging from buds everywhere. Steep forested hillsides tilt over me like delicate watercolors built from soft washes of green with hints and highlights of buttercup. The taunt of a lopsided moon disappears over the ridge. In a sky so blue you can almost see the night behind it, tattered clouds appear — breathtakingly white above, the color of pewter or sackcloth below. From their lairs on the slopes, four or five different kinds of birds sing — some songful, others nondescript but full of pep. Squirrels scamper up high. The smells in the air are of wild onion, spice-bush, pine needles, and damp earth. The nearby creek lollygags off round the next bend talking to itself.

My companions are up ahead somewhere. I can hear their footfalls shuffling through the leaves. We hunt the edible mushrooms of the Midwest spring. The tasty morels! Every spring in the Ozarks a two- or three-week season comes when country people have enough sense to drop whatever they are doing and head for the woods in search of these delectable inventions of the wild earth. Up early, we've been out for hours. My eyes weary of the hunt and my feet hurt already. Just as I decide to head back for the thermos full of hot coffee in the truck, I catch a tantalizing glimpse out of the corner of my eye. Could it be?

Heading for the base of a big sycamore on the other side of the creek, I step into chilly water that flows over my boot top soaking my socks. I see the first mushroom — elfin, pockmarked, and moistly fresh — poking up through the dew-sprinkled grass. Elated, I lift it gently from the leaf litter. As I place it in my plastic sack I see another peeking from around the side of the tree. And another. And then another. I have stumbled on a whole morel colony! Soon my bag is full — and so is my heart, with the ancient joy of the forager.

Walking back to join my friends, I feel good. I want to yell and dance. If Donald Trump offered

to trade places with me now, I'd turn that bally-
hooed billionaire down flat. Not all the money on
Wall Street, I believe, could begin to purchase a shred
of the unalloyed joy that warbles inside me. That
night the delight and excellence of the day is rekin-
dled as we cook up a dinner that centers around
the wild mushrooms. We stuff their hollow goodness
with garlic, fresh parsley, and ground pepper, with
egg, brown rice, and cheese. Someone brought some
honest homemade bread. We make up a salad, dress
it with lemon, olive oil, and fresh mint, and uncork
a bottle of wine. Our appetites honed to an edge by
a day of fresh air and exercise, that plate of food
loaded with stuffed wild mushrooms and fresh salad
is everything anyone could ever want from a dish —
even in a dream.

We talk the evening away over our empty plates
in that happy stew of congenial company wherein
you can speak of anything you please, peppered and
salted with lots of joking, laughing. Later I go outside for a walk. On a hillside caressed by night winds
and scented with mountain mint and azalea, I lie in
the damp spring grass and watch rags of sooty cloud
sail past the waning moon. Serenaded by the callings of whippoorwills and of owls interrogating the
darkness, I carefully wrap this day and store it in
memory's bulging treasure chest.

Thirsty in the Ocean

"My thanksgiving is perpetual," wrote Henry David Thoreau more than 150 years ago. "Oh how I laugh when I think of my vague indefinite riches. No run on my bank can drain it – for my wealth is not possession but enjoyment." The sage of Walden Pond alluded to the riches of this world we find ourselves in which then and now are well nigh inexhaustible. One notices time and again that, after all, we are extravagantly blessed with simple gifts. Consider as evidence the delight of mornings, the sparkle and glint of sun on newly minted leaves in the fever that is spring, the very common sight of blue skies overhead visited by shining galleons of cloud, the good smell of rain, the incensed breezes of summer. Have you noticed that the world is crammed with hoptoads and cat's tongues, with the painted curves, bends, and folds of flowers, the tang of apples, the lightfooted grace of running deer, the dazzle and twist of sleek leaping trout, the time-sculpted crags and wrinkled, wizened features of our glittery-eyed elders, the bony knees of towheaded children, the sweet, haunting incoherence of our own dreams? These treasures make wealthy tycoons of us all.

You don't have to be a nature lover either! City dwellers can easily locate treasure galore on mufflered midwinter walks down snow-hushed sidewalks when the street lights come on at four, humid summer evenings porch-sitting to the metronome blessing of cicadas, wet streets dazzle-painted with electric reflections after late evening rains, companionable dinners with loved ones in restaurant booths like friendly confessionals, the gee-whiz fulfillment walking home after a July 4th technicolor fireworks display down at the commons, walks in the fresh light and crisp air of autumn to the music of far-off playgrounds, browsing past serendipitous arrays in antique shop windows on Saturday afternoons, those bedazzled nights on the town you just want to go on and on, the energy and bustle of downtown sidewalks on weekday afternoons.

Kabir, a twelfth-century Indian mystic, once said, "I was surprised when I heard the fish in the ocean were thirsty!" Who among us has not felt like a beggar at a banquet — much too often too busy or distressed to stop and smell the roses in the great blessing of our backyards? I want to offer the ways of simple living as one method for us ocean-dwellers to quench our thirst.

For the world is afloat on the holy, crammed with the sacred, strewn and littered with beauty everywhere that is full of grace and with simple gifts that bespeak a hulking sly benevolence behind things. Most of us encounter moments that rumor and gossip of the goodness of our world, occasions when our hope and faith in life and in others are restored, when we sense a deep harmony behind things, when we sit and savor the mute blessedness of creation (and the vast mystery that underlies that blessing). Most enjoy the occasional mushroom hunt that turns out just right. Such excursions and encounters are the pulsing heartbeat of all the world's religions. Spirituality is, in part, the business of discovering and honoring those gifts and that mystery, those forays into blessing that fortify and nurture our wholeness.

The small personal computer on which I am typing bears a printed label that proclaims "Intel Inside." This refers to the processor (made by Intel), that tiny etched silicone chip inside the putty-colored terminal box on which the busy work of the computer gets done lightning fast. Every major religion in the world has a similar brand of processor inside it – the ways of spirituality offered to its followers. Spirituality is where the rubber hits the road, where the divine and the human interact in the business of everyday living, the interface of the inner and the outer. Spirituality is that internal processor that enables us to live deeply and well, to take in nourishment for our souls and to give out love. Spirituality begins when the twin mysteries of our fragile human hearts and the whispering voice of divinity meet.

The spirituality of simple living involves strategies to increase these moments of blessing in our lives, to *harvest* them and *harness* them to power our efforts to build a better life and a better world. What are some of those strategies? I offer three of them here – three paths down which to walk for a share in the adventure of simple and generous living. They are, first, the cultivation of *awe and wonder within us;* second, the cultivation of *the elected neediness or radical dependency of a poor life* that connects us with others, with community; and, third, the cultivation *of simple living as a spiritual rule,* a way of prayerful and hopeful living in chaotic and changing times.

Great Bulging Eyes

Let's begin down at the nearest pond. Ed Hays, founder of the Shantivanam prayer community in Kansas and spiritual writer, advises that we adopt the common frog as a mascot for this spirituality of simple living. The image of a frog could be hung on our walls as a religious icon, he suggests. One reason for doing so is that the frogs in our local ponds have great bulging eyes. We need that kind of eyes in order to live deeply and well. "To the eyes of the soul," Hays counsels, "everything is holy. Viewing life with the soul's enormous eyes allows us to see that we are swimming in the sacred!" With those great bulging soul eyes and a cultivated spirituality of simple living, we can backstroke through the holy, splash and delight in the taste of reality, find it easy both to pray always and to participate in the healing of our world. As theologian Monika Hellwig rightly claims, the primary issue in spirituality is not the redemption of the individual soul, but the redemption of our whole world.

Simple living can shape us into wide-eyed, loving, and earth-keeping people, such as scientist Loren Eiseley describes, "with just a touch of wonders in our eyes, a sense of marvel, a glimpse of what is happening behind the visible, who see the whole of the living world as though turning a child's kaleidoscope." Tall order? Kabir, that famous Muslim mystic, also said this: "When we say 'Ahhhhh!' and say it with a deep sigh" — the kind of exclamation that comes from our depths whenever we witness some aspect of the world's blessing, "that 'Ahhhhh' is one of God's most beautiful names." Each time you express that primal sound of wonder, know that you are announcing the presence of holy mystery in our midst. When we breathe out a heartfelt "Wow!" we are praying.

Father Thomas Berry, a recognized leader in the current eco-spirituality movement, styles himself a "geologian" (rather than a "theologian"). This means Berry builds his images of God and his spirituality from the ground up rather than from the top down. When asked what was the one most important element of a practical everyday spirituality of living, he answered with an intriguing word: "Enchantment." In order to engage in an active spirituality that makes sense, that works and is effective for our times, Berry urges the awakening of an energetic sense of awe and wonder within us. Enchantment comes as we see the whole universe, and especially the earth that gave us birth, as vast, sacred mysteries. We have been lost in the gaunt grip of a centuries-old split in our thinking and in our religious sense between the divine and the world, the sacred and the secular, the holy and the ordinary, the consecrated and the congregation, between heaven and earth, saint and sinner. In our day this profound split in our consciousness is beginning to heal, as we rediscover a more creation-centered view — one that recognizes the interconnectedness of all things and the nagging, pervasive presence of the divine mystery always and everywhere within our world.

Enchantment! It means being completely charmed by, bedazzled with, under the spell of the mystery and beauty in the world around us! The most healing of all emotions are awe and wonder. What's more, the altar rail that encloses the holy sanctuary runs clear around our whole planet. In the first book of the Old Testament we find Jacob exclaiming after an unexpected encounter with God in a dream: "Truly Yahweh is in this place and I never knew it! How awe-inspiring this place is! This is nothing less than a house of God; this is the gate of heaven." When we see this world as indeed holy ground, we take off our shoes and connect with a dynamic and transfiguring energy and will. The greatest scientist of our time, Albert Einstein, said this: "The most beautiful and powerful experience we can have is the encounter with mystery. It is the fundamental emotion that stands at the cradle of true science, true art, and true religion. Whoever does not know it is as good as dead, his eyes dimmed."

Matthew Fox, founder of the Institute in Culture and Creation Spirituality in California and another leader in the creation-centered spirituality movement, has expressed the various paths of this creation spirituality as commandments. These commandments are not so much imperatives for behavior as promises of rewards. If we look in these places, the commandments tell us, we will reap huge benefits for our living. The commandment connected with the very first path, what Fox calls the "Via Positiva," is this: *Thou Shalt Fall in Love at Least Three Times a Day.* This beginning path of creation spirituality calls us to awe and wonder, to enjoyment, to savor creation's simple pleasures, to hunt out and befriend beauty, to spend time with our friends, to celebrate our blessings and return thanks by passing them on to others. If we are ignorant of pleasure, Fox says, then we are ignorant of God. To know the divine and sacred, we must become ripe and juicy, delicious people, falling head over heels for the beauty and inner mystery of things around us on a regular basis. Three times a day our hearts should throb! What a prescription! – for falling in love kindles our passions and energies into flames. Falling in love is the way out of addiction, which is to fill the emptiness inside of us with things or with numbness instead of with beauty, passion, and fascination with the world around us.

Simple living is a way to clear the decks in order to diligently follow that first commandment. A wonderful parable for this dynamic of enchantment and blessing was the recent popular movie *Babette's Feast.* In that film, a sumptuous dinner carefully and lovingly prepared by a French refugee thawed the ice-cold heart of a Danish village into friendship and poignant forgiveness. The film showed the nearly miraculous healing power of simple good things.

But falling in love with beauty and grace, of course, is not enough. As we have noted, spirituality is about redeeming humanity and the planet, not just our individual souls. Blessings are abundant, but there is another side to our world as well – and we would be more than fools to ignore it.

Elected Neediness

Yesterday's paper lies on my desk. Far in the back is a news item describing a common event in our cities nowadays. In a poor neighborhood a man and woman are found shot to death. One circumstance screams its pity and horror even through the cold newsprint. The dead woman's two-year-old child was found in the morning wandering through the house wearing a diaper and soiled T-shirt. Police wrapped her in a blanket, it was reported, and handed her over to neighbors.

In the middle of the night I awake. It's again too warm for this time of year. I toss and turn in the close, humid dark while an old nursery rhyme echoes through my head.

Wee Willie Winkie runs through the town,
Upstairs and downstairs in his nightgown,
Rapping at the window, crying through the lock,
Are the children all in bed, for now it's nine o'clock.

Are the children all in bed? In this town last night there was one who wasn't. Now a disturbed and uneasy specter is rapping at my window, crying through my lock. Far off a siren wails like an awful banshee through the empty streets.

As I toss and turn in the night, I wonder. Is this report from one city's news that last straw, that tiny increment of weight that will finally tilt our teeter-totter irremediably one way rather than the other? It's very hard now, if not impossible, to foresee a future that is not crammed full with more bewildered children crying in empty houses. "The wasted and wandering lives," poet Dan Berrigan writes, "that meet our horrified gaze each day are a parable almost beyond bearing, a parable of our own condition. We too mourn. We too suffer. We too wander in a spiritual wasteland."

We play musical chairs with our poorest and neediest, leaving them to survive amid punishments and ruins. Our economics seems illuminated throughout by a dim bulb, the ethical vision of a strip-mine operator. We feed on our future greedily, thoughtlessly, taking and never giving back. Meaninglessness and destruction are as acceptable as anything else. The earth is at our mercy. Lamentations are in order. "This is not a time," adds Berrigan, "when great expectations make much sense."

As the Worldwatch Institute's Lester Brown patiently explains in his annual survey, *State of the World,* every living system on earth is in steep decline. The Institute recently released its report, which said our planet has at most only twenty years left before it completely collapses under the weight of human neglect and depredations. We must be near the point at which we must rise every day, very deliberately choose, and then strenuously work for a tomorrow that has a chance of being livable for our children.

Carol Lee Flinders, co-author of the very popular *Laurel's Kitchen* cookbooks, looks hard and reflects: "As I watch the breakdown of every 'fix' imaginable — technological, political, and economic — I am more, and more inclined to believe that the only real wild card in our affairs may be the human spirit itself." Thomas Merton wrote a year before he died, "Strange that the individual is the only power left. And though his power is zero, zero has great effect when one understands it and knows where to place it." Living lightly and generously on the planet and cultivating a spirituality of simplicity may be the well-placed zero, one of the keys to the incremental turnabout we need. If spirituality is about celebrating grace and bounty, it is also about making connections, knowing deep in our bones that we live in the midst of a great web — an infinitely complex network of interrelationships. On that vast web, action on one strand in turn affects many other strands as well. How we pluck those strands is important.

It is likely that there is a brutally direct connection between the newspaper headlines and the way we live our lives, between the suffering in our world, in our inner cities and out on our farms, and the profligate consumer way of living we have developed over the last generation. The paradox of our shopping mall–centered world is the parched and unloved life that waits for us at home. In spite of (or maybe because of) our many conveniences we seem stunted by our prosperity, autistic in our living. Further, our current wasteful and extravagant ways cannot be sustained without grave damage to the earth and without continually worsening deprivation for our fellow humans. We've all heard these comparative numbers: our little more than 6 percent of the world's population consumes 30 to 40 percent of its resources. We generate 25 percent of the world's pollutants and 30 percent of its garbage. Americans use twice as much energy per capita as other industrial nations with comparable standards of living, and ten to one hundred times as much as Third World nations. These numbers make us profoundly uneasy.

Close to home, surely the huge disparity between the cluttered garages and attics of our wealth and the living conditions of our poorest contributes substantially to the situations out of which rise the horrors in our daily headlines. How do we work toward a solution to these problems? What can we do in our own lives to begin to turn things around? Again, the spirituality of simple living provides a way, some choices.

The opposite of wealth is not poverty but sufficiency. It means having enough. Sufficiency is not a matter of sacrifice and deprivation; it is a means of working out different ways of achieving satisfaction in our own lives. Sufficiency is the concept that drives a simple and sustainable way of life. We've all seen the bumper sticker that reads, "Live Simply That Others May Simply Live" — a ringing call to a sustainable life. Such a life involves, in the words of Mennonite author Doris Janzen Longacre, "cultivating a gentle way of handling the earth, versatility in the face of shortage, inner provision for contentment and *more than all that,* commitment to live justly in our world." A sufficient and sustainable life means being a bright and creative part of the solution rather than one more tired cog in the dreadful turning wheels of the problems.

Sufficiency involves the virtues of thrift and frugality. Sustainability comes from innovation and creativity. It looks something like this. A friend reuses her bath and dishwater, hauling it out to the garden for her vegetables. It's a lot of bother, she says, but she doesn't mind. She gets exercise and cuts down on her water bill, while at the same time deriving a rich satisfaction from this way of living lightly on the earth. Once she drew the Green Triangle for me on a napkin. It looks like this:

Ecologist Ernest Callenbach devised this diagram to illustrate a principle of simple living. Anytime you do something beneficial for one point on the triangle, you also will almost inevitably do good for the other two. For example, suppose you decide to do something helpful for the environment: bicycling rather than driving your car on short trips. You thereby cut down pollution emissions, you reduce smog and lung damage, and you may help postpone the greenhouse effect. But you'll also help your health in the bargain because you get more regular exercise, and you'll also save a lot of money on gas, oil, and car depreciation.

I would go further to add a fourth point to Callenbach's triangle, label that point "Community," and make the Green Triangle into the Green Square. In addition to benefits for our budget, health, and the immediate environment, living lightly both eases the burden on the earth's resources and necessarily connects us directly and solidly with others. Simple living thereby becomes an energetic step toward a more just and equitable world, especially if we can utilize our own resources (time and money) to join in the struggle for a fairer distribution of the earth's limited resources. Living lightly can set us free to rebuild community, and, conversely, community can support us in our efforts at simple living.

By our sustainable way of living, our striving after sufficiency, we connect ourselves by means of strong cords to the community around us. Simple living can involve a kind of elected neediness and a radical dependency that invariably strengthens us and our communities together. Our culture directs us to engineer our total security, to surround ourselves with things and wealth, so that we are in no way ever dependent upon another. However, our spiritual traditions tell us that if we protect ourselves from insecurity, from vulnerability, we in turn cut ourselves off both from the Source, but also from the community we need in order to be fully human and compassionate. Franciscan preacher Father Richard Rohr has said: "One religion, Christianity, even dares to call God *a lamb.*" What is the nature of a lamb, if not simple, vulnerable, and dependent upon others? Spirituality often turns things upside down and inside out. To be human is to be insecure, dependent. Even God chose community – to be a weak and gentle lamb in our midst.

"The real meaning of a poor life," says Rohr, "is a life of radical dependency, so that I can't arrange my life in such a way that I don't need you." Less really is more. Dependency naturally leads to a sense of sufficiency, for accumulating or hoarding makes no sense when you know you *absolutely need other people* for your life to continue. This gospel call to elected neediness summons us to be satisfied less with material wealth and more with human community, with developing creativity, friends, with simple craft and art and making-do, with conversation, lovemaking and play together, knowing what is enough, knowing with certainty that we cannot live without others or thrive apart from the community of life on earth.

In his fabulous book *The Different Drum*, bestselling author M. Scott Peck investigates the subject of community-building. He concludes that "in and through community lies the salvation of the world. ... Through authentic community, we can make hope real again and make the vision of living peacefully together manifest in a world which has almost forgotten the glory of what it means to be human." It sounds like Peck idealizes the role of community, but he emphasizes over and over again that community-building is difficult, arduous, hard work plagued with hazard, that there is more *pain* in community – but also in the end more *joy*. We absolutely need the give-and-take of community in order to be fully alive, generously human, and able to live in simple ways.

Our modern culture has taught us that dependency on others, the need for friendship and community, are signs of weakness. Just think of one very popular cultural icon that we all grew up with – those characters Clint Eastwood has always played in films (either the Man with No Name or Dirty Harry). Tough, flinty-eyed, hard-jawed independent men, they would single-handedly restore order to one of our crime-afflicted communities and then ride off alone just before the closing credits, while the rest of us clutched each other in wimpy embraces.

Our spiritual traditions on the other hand tell us that dependency on others is a sign of strength. Indeed, in the Christian tradition and in its theology, even ultimate reality, the very ground and underlying matrix of being itself, the true source of all that is ... is, well, a community, a Trinity, three Persons who need one another. The central ritual of Catholic Christianity is the Eucharist, the breaking of bread together. Buddhist monks pray every day the words of the Buddha, "I seek refuge in the *Sangha* [the community of seekers]."

Elected neediness is a way of reflecting that ultimate design in our lives, of deliberately setting ourselves up for the pursuit of wholeness in the midst of community. If "enchantment" is one vital quality needed for spirituality in our day, then "intimacy" and "community" are the other two. For thousands of years now we humans have been moving toward increased isolation from one another. From big rowdy hunting-gathering tribes we went to an agricultural society in which groups huddled in villages. Then we moved into cities and huddled in neighborhoods. The extended family broke down, and then so did the nuclear one. With this progression to isolation, perhaps now we need a "Declaration of Dependence" to restore some much-needed balance after the long march toward independence.

It is no accident that in the midst of our consumer culture we live in such isolation. Ideally each one of us dwells in a separate housing unit. It's simply good for business when we all live apart from one another. When each of us must have her own auto, his own lawn mower, her own television, his own washer and dryer, then the cash registers are kept busy. But we pay a steep price in the coin of loneliness, alienation from one another, with elders who feel useless, with teenagers who have nothing really worthwhile to do with their time.

Household, neighborhood, and community have suffered terribly from this consumer-oriented design for living.

Experiments are beginning in various places around the world and here in the U.S. with creative alternatives to our isolated ways of living. In Denmark, for example, we have seen the rise of *bofaellesskaber* — co-housing communities in which people own their own homes but share mutual amenities built into the project. These might include gardens, a library, laundry, and workshops. Many of these projects have community dining — a boon for singles and seniors. Single parents can find child care easily, and kids are safer because cars are banished to peripheral parking lots. There is little crime, and co-housing is surprisingly affordable. "I know I live in a community," one resident of Trudesland, a community near Copenhagen said, "because on Friday night it takes me forty-five minutes and two beers to get from the parking lot to my front door."

We tend not only to isolation from one another, but also to estrangement from our own inner depths. A consistent theme in both feminist consciousness-raising and in the recent men's movement has been the need to reconnect with our insides, to discover intimacy with our deepest identity, with our own souls. Spirituality has always been about cultivating a rich inner life, together with a prayerful stance toward the outer. Simple living means to work for a life that is outwardly simple, but inwardly rich and sumptuous, full of inner provision for contentment. The spirituality of simple and generous living involves the care and feeding of a soul.

A Rule for Unique Amphibians

The pursuit of wholeness (holiness) and prayer, the cultivation of a soul, seem sometimes so irrelevant, unappealing, and impossible of achievement. Due to that split-asunder religious view from our past, that sense of a great divide between the holy and the ordinary and everyday, between those set apart for holiness and the rest of us, prayer and the cultivation of a rich inner life seem far out of reach to us. But we are healing this split and seeing our world as all of a piece with all of creation, a seamless fabric woven by a mystery that is both transcendent and immanent. That mystery is above all *diverse* and lives inside everything, as indeed all things live within the mystery. This means every living being and every nook and cranny around us is shot-through with the sacred and holy. Earth is crammed with heaven. Since the divine is within creation, then it follows that prayer, wholeness, and the journey into the soul are not supernatural achievements, but should be easy and available, second nature to us all. Spirituality is really our natural element.

Ed Hays again refers to those common mascots for our spiritual living: "You and I are like frogs," he says. "We were created to swim in the sacred as well as to live in the world. We're unique amphibians to whom both the sacred and the secular are natural." Spiritual-ity then is not something "extra" added on to the rest of our life, nor is it reserved for an elite. "Spirituality is not," writes Brother David Steindl-Rast, "a special department; it is just a higher intensity of aliveness. ...Since life is of one piece, one's inner aliveness must express itself in outer aliveness." Jesus him-self in the gospels says that he came to bring life in abundance to everyone – nothing more, nothing less.

One of the foremost Christian theologians of our century, Karl Rahner, remarked once that if our reli-gions do not reconnect with their mystical traditions and offer us a dynamic and practical spirituality that is relevant to our ordinary living and that connects us in real and meaningful ways with divine mystery, then these religions have *absolutely nothing to offer us* as we near the end of the twentieth century.

In mid-May of the year 1373 the woman who would later compose the first book ever written in the English language died at the tender age of thirty-one... or so her bedside companions thought. In the throes of a severe respiratory infection, this middle-class English woman, Julian by name, experienced what we call today a "near death experience." In vi-sions like those of the star-traveler in *2001: A Space Odyssey,* she navigated the galaxies, up and down the wide corridors of the universe, crying out *Benedicite* in bewildered fear and dread. Through the vast, wounded heart of our world, she journeyed to a beautiful and shining city, which it turned out was located within her own soul. There, in hushed awe and breathless wonder, she saw the divine mystery personified, the Holy One – whom she described as, curiously enough, a bit homely, but also most courteous and personable. The Divine Sustainer held the whole universe (it looked like a little wrinkled hazelnut) in warm, caring hands – loving it, suffering along with it, bathing it in kindness and love.

Shortly after experiencing this life-changing vision, Julian moved into a small cell attached to the church at Norwich and spent the rest of her life in prayer and giving spiritual direction. A contemporary of Chaucer, she recorded her visions in a book that she called *Revelations of Divine Love.* Her simple advice to all who came to her seeking guidance and wisdom: "It's going to be all right, folks. All shall be well, and all manner of things shall be well." When seekers asked her how they should live in the meantime, she answered: "Live kindly!"

Julian's remarkable visions occurred smack in the middle of the High Middle Ages, the thirteenth and fourteenth centuries, wherein occurred what historian of spirituality Richard Woods calls "a mystical revolution." In those troubled times there took place a great renewal of spirituality in the Western world. Prior centuries saw the rise of monasteries, those great Benedictine, Augustinian, Cistercian, and Carthusian institutions that preserved learning and civilization through the dark times after the collapse of the Roman empire and the barbarian attacks on Europe. Monastic orders provided written "rules" for those attracted to their life, instructions from the founder that organized, governed, and shaped the monk's effort to weave spirituality into daily living. The rule for Benedictines, for example, favored prayer and work in equal measures. Discipline and hospitality to others were also emphasized. The Carthusian rule became the most austere of all, espousing strict solitude, silence, abstinence, and contemplative retirement from the world. Monasteries endured and prospered for centuries, a central fixture in and support of the medieval culture.

By the end of the twelfth century, however, there was great ferment and unrest in Europe. The primary "ism" of the day, feudalism, had passed. The rise of the middle class and an increase in urban population occurred. These were times of ghastly institutional decadence and breakdown and an abrupt widening of the rift between the haves and the have-nots. Swings in climate brought about crop failures and famines. Radical and apocalyptic religious ideas and cults flourished and won converts. Such was the air of despair and social disintegration current that religious cults like the Cathars attracted followers by the hundreds of thousands. These sects believed that the world was so blighted with evil and doomed that it would be a grave sin to bring children into it. Parades of flagellants roamed the countryside, doing penance to atone for free-floating guilt and remorse. These were the centuries of the Black Plague, when a third of the population of Europe died in horrible agony, and of the Hundred Years War between the superpowers of the day, France and England.

While a period in history of great torment and turmoil, it was also a time of great hope and creative vision. Spiritual seekers, disenchanted with both the corrupt religious institutions and the radical alternative cults of the day, turned within to their own experience for vision and guidance. This inner searching bore great fruit. It led to the rise of the mendicant orders, the Dominicans and the Franciscans. Francis of Assisi, a sensitive youth greatly troubled by the insanity, greed, and heartlessness of his times, looked deeply within his own experience, listened attentively to his dreams, paid attention to his heart's longings. Kindled into white-hot passion, Francis married the medieval ideals of courtly love and chivalry to gospel spirituality and his love affair with "Lady Poverty." The creative result was the founding of the famous Franciscan order. Francis of Assisi devised a new way to live a life devoted to service, prayer, and poverty, one that immediately caught on and attracted the commitment of many followers.

During this time also, a widespread lay movement of working-class women emerged. These women called themselves Beguines. They were profoundly religious, yet were neither nuns nor recluses, choosing to live in the world according to a simple gospel spirituality. The Beguines were a lay movement, full of remarkably strong women who embraced a life of voluntary poverty, prayer, and service of the poor, the sick, the suffering. Many Beguines supported themselves with handiwork, particularly weaving, spinning, and sewing, making lace and other crafts. They gave any surplus income to the poor. To our own day, traces of this movement survive in the term "spinster" applied to older, unmarried women. These medieval women formed communities known as "Beguinages," some of which still exist in Belgium today.

The Beguines have been called the first women's movement in Western history. Here women banded together to dedicate their lives to spiritual development and service to others through ministry and spiritual direction. Like Francis, they looked deep within their own souls for the spiritual authority that they failed to find in the pulpits and doomsday cults that surrounded them. Beguine women honored their own experience and their inner voices, dreams, and visions. They formed the first Christian "base communities." Many of them with a bent for it deliberately cultivated mystical experience and then wrote about the results, making their wisdom available to others. Julian of Norwich was an example of this mystical searching. Beguine mystics played a central role in the return of the feminine face of the divine to Western religion, in devising new devotions and pieties for the common folk. The Catholic feast of Corpus Christi was inaugurated by Beguines.

Together these remarkable women accomplished a great quantum leap forward in spirituality (one we even now have not completely explored or digested). They found new ways to understand a God who is present within creation. They built rainbow bridges between the inner life and the outer. They squarely faced the challenges presented to them by the anguished times in which they lived. Their accomplishment also involved much creative innovation, with the invention of new and satisfying ways to live in the midst of turbulent and changing times. Beguine women helped move their world forward out of chaos and loss of meaning into new vitality and direction.

We can learn much from our past. Many today are yearning for a different way to live, a sacred way of existing on the earth. In our day, the disciplines and creativity of a spirituality of simple living can serve us in much the same way they served medieval men and women looking for guidance and wholeness in the midst of chaotic, rapidly changing times. In the Middle Ages spiritual seekers were faced with the urgent need to look deeply and honestly within themselves for creative innovation and solutions, to bond together in strong and loving communities for support, and to embrace poverty and concern for others as a kind of rule for their lives. In effect, people like the Beguines and Francis of Assisi mounted a proactive assault on the pain, despair, and hopelessness of their times.

It is up to you, the reader, to judge whether or not we could greatly profit from similar strategies for our lives as we near the end of the twentieth century. In our day we suffer from rampant epidemics of child abuse, sexual violence, crime, oppression, despair, loss of meaning, and grave and even irreversible harm to the earth. If we are to navigate our culture successfully past the reefs of social break-down and the shoals of environmental catastrophe into the next millennium, we could do worse than profit from the experience of those who have gone before, women and men who bravely and imagina-tively faced similar challenges.

Take just one increasingly urgent challenge we face in our living nowadays – our work. Since techno-logical innovations like computers are effecting great changes in our economy, we are moving rapidly to-ward a time when our human material needs can be met by the labor of a small fraction of our popu-lation. Important questions that loom in our future most probably will be similar to these:

- How much work is there?

- Is there enough to go around?

- How do we divide this work among us?

- Since we largely define ourselves by and find our self-worth in the work we do, how can we feel worthy and good about ourselves if we are not "working"?

The work ethic served us well during the industrial era when we were building our immense capital and technological base, but it may now be blocking our ability to redefine ourselves within a whole range of human activity. Here is an area of great challenge, one that will demand creative solutions. Our survival as a healthy people and as a democracy may very well depend on reinventing ourselves, finding other ways to be fulfilled outside of work and career. The cultivation of spirituality in a simple and prayerful life, the good work of crafting a soul may well be one of those other ways that attracts and guides many of us toward a productive alternative.

The art, science, and adventure of simple living can provide all the ingredients of a dynamic and practical spirituality for everyday living: a way to pray, a way to be mindful, a way to fully enjoy and celebrate the blessings of life, a way of self-surrender and emptying, a way of offering our lives toward a higher purpose, a way of connecting and strengthening the bonds with others in good communities, a way of service and generosity, a way of humility, and a mystical way. Simple living can provide the framework of a rule for weaving spirituality into our living. Just as monastic rules and those of the mendicant orders shaped and guided the daily living of monks in the cloisters and friars in the cities, so the ways of simple living can serve us in our daily living during the 1990s and beyond.

An important element of all spiritual rules was provision for setting aside time to pray and meditate. The choices involved in seeking a simpler life can free up that time for us. Self-denial was a part of ancient rules, as was the cultivation of solitude and spiritual reading. These can easily be incorporated into efforts toward living lightly. Good work and community-building were essential elements of most monastic rules, and they are equally vital to the

ways of simple living. The rigors of spiritual discernment will be familiar to anyone who has attempted to
make wise choices in our day of endless variety and
infinite options. The old disciplines of fasting and
sabbath-keeping also carry over rather well. In a wide
variety of ways monastic and other spiritual rules en-
couraged the development of prayer and a rich inner
life connected in a practical manner with the Divine
Mystery. Every available tool of soul-craft was called
into play. Rules were also designed to nourish within
that soul a solid and unshakeable faith.

The spirituality of simple living is about cultivating that rich and fertile inner life by emptying
ourselves outwardly so that we can savor and be
made whole by prayer and by the goodness, blessings, and grace in our world. The ways of simple
living can lead to an energetic faith, because living
lightly on the earth above all is *praise*. Simple living returns homage to creation. The Jewish spiritual
leader Rabbi Abraham Heschel said, "Praise precedes
faith." The beauty and blessings in our world elicit
that praise a thousandfold; we praise and celebrate
what is good and beautiful and bountiful. This grateful homage is the starting point for faith, because
faith is not really about correct belief and dogmas.
True faith is trusting that the whole universe is a feast
of blessing and that the world we live in is a generous gift, created – as it says in Genesis – by a Deep
Mystery who found that creation very good.

Faith gathers evidence from our life experiences
and from our spiritual traditions. Faith relies on the

affirmative answers to these questions: Is the unfath-
omable craft that fashioned the universe illumined
within by mighty and unquenchable light? Wrapped
within darkness deeper than all of winter's mid-
nights, enfolded within the riddles of the heavens
and of nature, can it be that there are huge secrets
that hide real surprises in store for us, a porch light
or two left on, maybe even a cosmic Cheshire-cat–
like smile that betrays a never-ending generosity and
love? These are the questions answered by a faith that
is enchanted with many-splendored rumors of eternity and intimate with a loving Creator who quietly
beckons and asks us to "Live kindly!"

The Joys of Tightwaddery

The last several years have seen an increase in attention to the ways of simple living. Alternatives to
overly consumptive lifestyles are fast becoming a hot
item on the mainstream ticket. You may have noticed
that bookstores are stacked high with earth-keeping
books these days, books that list hundreds of ways
to be good to the planet, most of them involving
choices that lead to a simpler lifestyle. As far back
as 1975, a Harris poll indicated that 77 percent of
Americans were willing to shift their lifestyles toward simpler ways. In 1991 *Time* magazine featured
the trend toward simpler living on a cover, heralding
it as the "way of the '90s." The editor of a popular
newsletter called *The Tightwad Gazette: Promoting*

Thrift as a Viable Alternative," Amy Dacyczyn, who lives in Maine, has attracted a lot of media attention. Every month this publication shares ideas on living frugally. The editor promotes "tightwaddery" as an attitude toward life that leads to both benefits for the environment and financial independence, debunking the common notion that the way to save more is to earn more.

In my own moderate-sized city in the last eight years or so, I have seen several ongoing support groups emerge for people who seek simpler ways of living. One community university course a few years ago called it "applied ecology." That same catalog was full of courses on solar and wind-generated power, organic gardening, composting, sun ovens, home bicycle repair, beer and wine making, sewing, gourmet cooking classes, sessions on meditation, centering, and spirituality in general, on home schooling and home birth, rebuilding community, alternative politics, edible landscaping, right livelihood, bioregionalism... you name it! A huge effort seems to be underway everywhere to turn our living around toward wiser choices. I want to call attention to three characteristics of this recent burgeoning of the simple living movement that seem to me especially hopeful, a sign that this trend is a very healthy and robust one and here to stay.

First, the simple living movement is an alternative approach characterized by *an attitude of taking direct personal responsibility for the social and environmental predicaments in which we find our-*

selves. There is an emphasis throughout on making connections between local conditions and global issues. The motto for this attitude, of course, is "Think Globally, Act Locally." Often this translates into a return to a real grassroots democracy and activism. We link hands, minds, computers, and financial resources to effect needed change in our local community, to lobby for the installation of an efficient city-wide recycling program, for instance. We take heart from an oft-quoted statement from Margaret Mead: "Never doubt that a small group of thoughtful, committed citizens can change the world. Indeed, it is the only thing that ever has."

In some cases, persons committed to this local activism have run for office as a way to further influence public policy. This heralds a slow but positive move away from our plutocratic (rule by the wealthy) form of government, from even what an editor of *Whole Earth Catalog* calls "kakistocracy" — government by a society's worst elements. Indeed, when politics itself is unhooked from human values and from spirituality, then those least qualified to run our public affairs will be the ones who are in office. The world applauded the people of the former Czechoslovakia when they elected a writer and poet, Vaclav Havel, as their president. Havel himself said, "If *everyone* doesn't take an interest in politics, it will become the domain of those least suited to it." Further, the 1992 Summit on the Environment in Brazil made newsworthy the worldwide emergence of Non-Governmental Organizations (NGOs) as the principal power behind the global effort to save the environment. People at the grassroots are making a difference all around the globe.

Second, there is *an ongoing exploration of and emphasis on "appropriate" use of technology*. Although a bumper sticker urging us "Back to the Pleistocene!" does exist (promoted by the radical extreme in the environmental movement), only a few want to turn back the clock of human development and return to the ways of our hunting-gathering ancestors or even to the much simpler tools and methods of a hundred years ago. Our technology is a terribly mixed bag, but most agree that by and large it is a blessing when it relieves us from much suffering and drudgery. The criterion for deciding on technology's use seems to be whether that technology is *appropriate*, whether it supports a sustainable life, and whether, in the end, it causes more good than harm. This judgment must be made on a case-by-case basis. The emphasis is away from blind worship of technology toward asking hard and wide-ranging questions first, weighing the benefits with the hazards in light of our best human values and priorities.

A family I know with two teenagers live deep in the Missouri Ozarks on a farm far from the power lines. There are, though, no smoky kerosene lanterns dangling from their rafters, no buckets of bathwater warming on their woodstove. Without electric bills, relying on a few solar panels to power their limited needs, the privation and makeshift lifestyle one would imagine go along with off-the-power-grid living are conspicuously absent. A small research business keeps them supplied with the limited cash they need to survive. In order to maintain that business successfully the use of a small personal computer is necessary. The computer is run off the solar-supplied batteries. They have no television, but do have a small cassette player for music. The thick walls of their owner-built house are super-insulated. This, combined with south-facing windows and water circulating from a rooftop heater, allow them to heat their home with only a small amount of wood each year. All in all this seems to me the kind of appropriate use of technology that makes sense.

Third, there is *the conviction that living a sane, generous, and ecologically responsible life does not mean self-sacrifice, privation, and austerity. On the contrary it should mean a richer, more interesting, more creative, fuller, longer, and healthier life.* It is a living, breathing rambunctious paradox, but all manner of good things emerge from the dynamics of simple living. It can be a lot of fun, even an adventure. Indeed if we are going to build a sustainable society for the future, one in which every act is inherently restorative and brings our commerce and government into alignment with the natural world and with human values, then the ways and means by which we accomplish this huge task must be widely engaging, even to some extent fun. The endeavor must contain the elements of great adventure.

The folks who are involved with these alternative ways recognize that the solutions to our problems are not simple; they are difficult, messy, and incremental. Uncounted ignorant personal acts brought us to the present situation; countless personal actions of a well-informed and energetic citizenry are the only way out. Are there flaws and mistakes made in these actions and efforts? Of course there are. Welcome to Planet Earth! But those committed to taking these actions seem to be spirited ones, full of hearty energy and creativity, imagination and humor. They seem to be unflinching in their willingness to look at, discuss, and deal with the monumental problems that face us as the century ends. By and large, they are lively and interesting people, committed to making the kinds of changes that will provide a sustainable future for their children and grandchildren.

Quite simply, the rewards of generous and simple living are life in abundance.

❀

Late that April night after the mushroom hunt, I lay waiting for sleep in my bed near an open window. Nestled under warm covers and weary with the sweet languor that comes from good work done in fresh air, I turned to watch the commonplace spectacle of midnight outside.

In the Ozark dark a chill had risen from the lower depths of the hollow and hushed the tree frog chorus. The whippoorwills quit their rapid-fire callings long ago. Out in the forest, talons are sheathed, lustings are stilled, nightwings are folded up in this mute stronghold of quiet. Storm clouds, thunder and lightning lodge for the night far over the ridges at the beck and call of daybreak. The racing pulse of spring is paused. Now a silence that is more like a presence broods and dreams in the pine-scented air.

Up in the dark sublime above, silhouettes of the oak branches divide and section the landscape of constellations into rough-edged fragments and shards. Twinkling in aloof passion, the stars look like connect-a-dot hieroglyphs written by some long-forgotten race of glittery-eyed beings, spelling out wise and abstruse theories beyond imagining up in the high balconies and lofts of the sky. Ascending and descending, the Milky Way circles the slumbering earth. The vast vault above seems nothing more nor less than an epochs-old cathedral filled with votive candles and praiseful liturgies, pure ablutions poured out by worshipful celebrants.

Teresa of Avila once said she was so grateful for her life and the world she could be bought with a sardine. This moment I know what she meant. I'd go for a song myself.

Thanksgiving wells in me for the blessing of this common night, for my family and friends, for the twistings and turnings of my life. Gravity itself seems a grace. The dark, I know, will pass and the hills will rise again out of the shadows in the modest pageantry of the morning after this nightly benediction.

My prayer rises with all the others. Let me rise up tomorrow and every day like new bread. Let me speak well of this place, this beautiful earth, and let me live simply and generously in its midst.

Chapter 3

The Great Balancing Act

STEVEN SPIELBERG, the filmmaker whose credits include blockbusters like *ET, The Color Purple*, and *Jurassic Park,* was being interviewed. A critic had panned his films because of excessive references to other movies. Spielberg's reply: "Of course, he's right. That's all I know. I grew up in the suburbs, and all I ever did was watch movies. Then I started making them. I never had a life."

He spoke of his admiration for Hollywood director John Huston, who made such cinema masterpieces as *The African Queen, The Maltese Falcon,* and *The Treasure of the Sierra Madre*. Before he became a film director, Spielberg noted, Huston had worked variously as a longshoreman, a roustabout in the southwest oil fields, and even a stint as a bouncer in a Mexican brothel. In short, he had wide experience of life under his belt. Spielberg felt this showed up in spades in his work. Huston's movies stood on their own, redolent with evocative mood, inventive camera work, sprightly dialogue, and too busy telling a whopper of a tale to have time to refer to other films.

Teenagers, those perennial fonts of wisdom, often express themselves in timely and insightful clichés. One of my favorites is the exhortation, "Get a life!" It's good advice, especially for those concerned about simple living. Since lifestyles are an outward expression of inner values, in order to live simply and generously we must pay close attention to our inner spiritual reality. How do we find the way to divine mystery and then how do we connect with it? Just living a life, with all its challenges, rewards, and ups and downs, is an engaging and productive spiritual path.

Because of that point of view from times past that is too otherworldly and disembodied, God's immanence within creation has long been neglected in favor of God's transcendence. It's probably a big reason why we trash the planet like we do, and it shows up in our thinking about who and what is holy. Our popular image of a holy person, someone intensely living a spirituality, has long been of someone withdrawn from the world, a loincloth-clad guru meditating alone in a cave somewhere, a monk cloistered away in silence. But this image is gradually, and rightfully, changing to that of a person hip-deep in reality with her sleeves rolled up: a social worker surrounded by the homeless of the inner-city, a volunteer slain by death squads in the middle of Central American poverty, a white-and-blue-robed nun mopping the brow of a dying sidewalk-dweller in Calcutta, a protestor splashing blood on a missile silo in the Midwest.

And that life we live, that true spiritual path, need not always be packed with round-the-clock toil and service. Pat Livingston, a sought-after speaker at ministry conferences, recalls the time she gave the keynote address at a New York City gathering. Afterward in the reception line, a man asked her what she was going to do with her time in the Big Apple. "Prepare my next talk," she answered. "What!" he gasped. "You're smack in the center of world civilization with art galleries, museums, restaurants, and theater that are all once-in-a-lifetime experiences (not to mention the chance to watch the sunset over the ocean from the top of the World Trade Buildings), and you're going to lock yourself in a room with a speech!" He's right, she thought, and out she went for a day on the town that would glow in the photo album of her memories.

Living automatically provides the challenges we need to further our spiritual development. Father Ed Hays from the Shantivanam prayer community asks us to think about the Rent-a-Wolf plan, an old bit of folk spiritual wisdom. This plan maintains that if there is no wolf at your front door, you should hire one to come and howl at your doorstep. "Life is trouble, and trouble holds the magic to bring us together or destroy us," says Father Ed. "Troubles can bring forth greatness from us, heroism as well as creativity, or it can breed self-pity, bitterness, and a host of other evils. When our work and life in general is going smoothly, how easily we tend to forget about others who are in need....By sharing in the holy communion of trouble, we become bonded more tightly together as members of one great family." Perhaps this is why Jesus himself enrolled the rich of his time in the Camel-through-the-Needle's Eye Club — through their affluence they were able to avoid much of that holy communion of trouble.

Psychiatrist M. Scott Peck's very popular bestseller *The Road Less Traveled* begins with this sentence: "Life is difficult." Since life, as we all know, is usually a lot of trouble, it follows that in living one automatically reaps the benefits of Hay's Rent-a-Wolf Plan. Every day we sit at the table where the holy communion of trouble is shared. If we could run off to meditate in a cave in the Himalayas, navel-gazing till the sacred cows came home, we'd confront few hassles, only washing out our loincloths from time to time, but we would also likely not make much spiritual progress. And our easily won serenity would probably be shattered into pieces by the first wailing two-year-old or neurotic, freeloading panhandler that shuffled our way.

Gloria Davis teaches Native American spirituality in Santa Fe, New Mexico. Her notions about spirituality were first formed as she grew up in her traditional Navajo family. "I noticed," she told me, "that the holy people in our community, the ones we all turned to for spiritual guidance, the ones who conducted

the elaborate sings, blessing ceremonies, and healing rituals, were always the people who had the
keenest sense of humor. You could always tell them
by their laugh wrinkles." What an idea! The hall-
mark of holiness here is not a gaunt, hollow-cheeked
face or a look of other-worldly serenity, but just a
common, garden-variety lively sense of humor. And,
surely, laugh wrinkles have rarely been developed in
a cave or cloister. A sense of humor is perhaps chiefly
woven of the fabric of life's ups and downs, its absurdities and sorrows, its humdrums, its joys and
comical interludes, its tedium, tensions and ironies,
its unpredictable encounters and quiet satisfactions.

Meister Eckhart, medieval mystic, said that God is
tickled through and through when one of us man-
ages, in the midst of our difficult lives, to show some
compassion, to do an unrewarded kindness for another. I like that idea of a higher power. So make God
smile. Be kind to one another. Make God laugh and
laugh in delight. Get a life!

Then what? After I get myself a life, what do the
spiritual wise ones counsel me then to do? Well, listen
to that life, they say, and take spiritual direction from
it. Listen especially to your loves and passions.

They Shout; I Follow

My oldest friend Paige was always fascinated by the
sea, its lure and lore. When he was a kid, model ships
cluttered his room, posters of sail and nautical charts

papered the walls. He read every book he could find about sailing and would rhapsodize about this passionate love and his dreams until we his friends got the picture.

The picture looked like this: Paige on the slippery deck of a battered but sturdy sailboat making its way slowly through an agitated sea under a dark, threatening sky. He is busy reefing the sails and securing thick, sodden lines on the deck, making the vessel ready to endure a storm. One arm flung across the sun-cracked paint on the mast, his hands wrapped in the rigging, he surveys the heaving, leaping surface of the sea ahead with steady, glittering eyes.

As happens to us all, adult responsibilities eroded his passion to a hobby. But Paige takes his dreams seriously. A persistent lament for his unrealized vision of living to the fullest once broke shackles. He ached for the opportunity now and then for the blood to sing in his veins, for his heart to pound and strain against rawborn winds and tides, for his courage and resourcefulness to be tested out in the cloud-shrouded Pacific dark. So one day he ordered plans by mail, rented space at the marina in Oakland where he lived, bought materials. Then, in his spare time, he built a boat — a twenty-six-foot cruising trimaran, to be exact. He named her *Heart of Gold* after a Neil Young song. He could sail only on weekends, but sail his elegant craft he did.

That's not the end of the story. Today Paige earns his living as a ship builder and, I believe, he's a fortunate man.

"By the time many people are fourteen or fifteen," mused science fiction writer Ray Bradbury, "they have been divested of their loves, their ancient and intuitive tastes, one by one, until they reach maturity, and there is no fun left, no zest, no gusto, no flavor." Reflecting on his long career as a writer, Bradbury claimed zest, gusto, and flavor were alive and kicking in his life because he was above all a hostage — hostage to his passion and love. "You see, my stories have led me through my life. They shout. I follow. They run up and bite me on the leg.... Then, when I finish, the idea lets go and runs off."

The end result was a life lived as a fascinating adventure.

"Follow your bliss," advised Joseph Campbell in his famous interviews with Bill Moyers, stressing the importance to the spiritual life of cultivating our unique interests, passions, and loves. In what do you most delight? Where is your heart of hearts? To what does your body and soul wholeheartedly want you to go? What keeps you fresh and eager? What makes you most enthusiastic? Campbell's bliss happened to be studying world mythology. Sail and the sea were Paige's deepest loves. Yours might be growing orchids, reading good mysteries, quilt-making, home schooling your kids, union organizing, mastering the dulcimer and playing in a bluegrass band, ballroom dancing, collecting Hummel dolls, finding and listening to vintage jazz recordings, writing haiku poetry, constructing your own log house, teaching fourth grade, grassroots political activism, refurbishing old Harley Davidsons, your current ministry (lucky you!), contemplatively walking, the Grateful Dead, starting recycling in your neighborhood, fine liturgy, photography, achieving justice in Central America or in your own workplace or in your own family, gardening, cooking and eating fiery Cajun dishes – you name it. You know.

Campbell compared what happens when one follows one's heart to a favorite image from the Middle Ages, that of the wheel of fortune. "There's the hub of the wheel," he said, "and there is the revolving rim. If you are attached to the rim of the wheel, you will be either always above going down or at the bottom coming up. But if you are at the hub, you are in the same place all the time, at the center."

That center where dwell our enthusiasms and deep gladness is the way our yearning to create finds expression in each and every one of us. In each one of us this expression is absolutely unique. When we find and poke at it, that touch is like probing a fat, throbbing nerve crammed full of joy and happiness. Channeled through our deepest loves, this urge to create comes from the source of our existence. We must again ask ourselves, who is the Creator? God is not a being who exists among other beings, but is the origin of all that exists, encompassing everything though not outside anything. The divine mystery remains incomprehensible, yet also knowable and revealed in many ways – in the natural world, in scripture, in the living of our lives, and particularly in our passions and delights.

Christianity is a religion of sacrament and incarnation, meaning that the Creator and Sustainer acts in every human life. "The reign of God," Jesus said, "is within you" (Luke 17:21). Could it be that divine mystery is with us *especially* at the level of our unique one-of-a-kind individuality? It makes sense, and this idea is even built into our language. Where do we find ourselves most unique, most one-of-a-kind? In those places within us that give birth to *enthusiasm*. The word "enthusiasm" literally means "God in us." Divine life is found most surely in our joys and true delights, and in the zestful, flavorsome adventure that comes when we follow those passions. "True prayer," says Father Richard Rohr, "is finding out who we are in God, finding the spacious place of the soul where we and God most feel at home." Observe your life diligently. Frequent encounters with deep gladness are a sign you are living fully and fruitfully your creativity.

Cultivating a spirituality for simple living involves locating and exploring those places in our soul that ring like great jubilant wind chimes to the breezes and whispers of the divine. Simplicity clears the decks for this vital work. It frees us from clutter so that we can wake up to and hear the great chiming within us.

One can easily thrash around aimlessly or become lost in the fog or becalmed and drifting in the spiritual life. There are so many choices, false trails, and dead ends. The recent conflagration in Waco, Texas, and lesser instances of fanatical religious fundamentalism point up the tragedies that follow when the inner life is silenced and we're cut off from the guiding gyroscope of our own souls, from our enthusiasm, from God hard at work deep within us. We become vulnerable to manipulation and especially to the pat answers of bad religion. Joseph Campbell suggests that a reliable guide through the labyrinths is that which brings a flush to our cheeks and a spring to our step. Campbell identified this bliss-following as "the soul's high adventure." Michelangelo called it "seeking the image in the heart." Following our deep gladness can give rise to a sensitivity to what is right and true, an inner balance, a tool for navigation through the shoals and reefs, currents and storms of lives that are always difficult.

Is this captivating dictum to follow our hearts just an excuse for self-indulgence? In the morning paper a columnist laments the lack of civility in our town. "We've turned into a nation of piranhas and slobs," he writes, "and it began when we started thinking that consideration for others isn't important and that doing your own thing is the highest goal in life." He raises a good question: When does bliss-following turn into mere self-indulgence? Is it nothing more than a kind of cheap grace? Perhaps the answer lies in the difference in verbs, between "do" and "follow." To just do your thing is to exercise and gratify your will at the moment, while following is a lifelong commitment and discernment and . . . well, there's no telling where you'll go. It is after all an adventure! Your love might very well take you to some places you'd rather not go. A passion for justice causes, for example, might lead to hard jail time. "Drunk with life," Bradbury describes it, "and not knowing where off to next. But you're on your way before dawn. And the trip? Exactly one-half terror, exactly one-half exhilaration."

Father Thomas Berry asks, "Can we have healthy humans living on a sick planet?" What separates authentic bliss-pursuing from self-gratification perhaps has to do with the ways in which our creative efforts and bearing fruit benefit others, help foster and support the health of our communities, in fact, the well-being of the whole earth community. "Neither the hair shirt nor the soft berth will do," wrote Frederick Buechner. "The place God calls you to is that place where your deep gladness and the world's deep hunger meet." Campbell's life work, for example, opened the doors for many to the richness and excitement of exploring the collective religious experience of the human race. After Moyers's interviews appeared on TV, discussion groups sprang up everywhere. People got excited, looking at their faith from a new perspective. Campbell's deep love helped all of us find deeper meaning and adventure in our living. Your bliss, your deep gladness has its roots both in heaven and deep within the human community.

We are back to that dance whose partners are inner smiling and outgoingness of heart.

Listening to Your Life

Locating our bliss and exploring our deep gladness are key landmarks in our individual spiritual journey. Other important events include those encounters with the divine mystery that enchant us and spur us on, together with the arduous growth that happens as we honestly struggle with the challenges life sets in our way. These are all elements that make up an inner life. These are important efforts in the business of crafting a soul and of living simply and generously. Psychiatrist Gerald May points out in his bestselling books (*Addiction and Grace, Simply Sane, The Awakened Heart,* to mention three) that excessive consumerism and burdensome addictions have such a tight stranglehold on us because of the current neglect of this inner work of building a human soul. In order to live beyond addictions and compulsive shopping, Dr. May prescribes the ways of spirituality. He calls it "the life of the heart."

Currently there is a widespread fascination with the elements of Native American spirituality. A central component of these spiritualities is the vision quest, that part of a native person's development in which he or she goes out into the wilderness for a period of time to fast and pray, to nourish an intimacy with the inner deeps, and to find direction for life. Ordinarily the regimen of the quest would give rise to vivid dreams or showings or visions. The quester would take these events back to the wise ones in the community for interpretation and counsel.

The irresistible fascination with these Native American ways seems to come from the refreshing fact that they honor, respect, and pay attention to our unique individual experiences. What occurs in a person's life — his or her inner stirrings, promptings, enthusiasms, relationships, struggles, trials, explorations, homecomings, defeats, and victories — are *primary* in native spirituality. Who each person is takes on great importance. Often a native person derived his or her very name from some important life experience. In this kind of spirituality, one navigates a course through life by heeding and honoring one's unique, individual experience and then by taking that inner life to the community's spiritual tradition in order to test its validity and to find counsel in its wisdom. One's own story is fitted into the larger story of the community. One's own life journey is a *gift* to that community that must be honored and used for the common good.

Francis of Assisi was wont to pray for nights on end, "Who are you, God, and who am I?" He was unable to find satisfying answers to his questions in the culture and institutions of his times. One Sunday he was listening to a sermon in which the preacher quoted Jesus telling his followers to take nothing for their journey, to rely upon the kindness of strangers — in short, to embrace poverty. Francis was galvanized. He left mass overjoyed and committed the passage to memory, saying: "This is what I want. This is what I long for. This is what I desire to do with all my heart." Francis had noticed that whenever and wherever he encountered poverty and simplicity in his life, then his heart would warmly glow, his insides would light up with smiles. The scripture passage validated this important inner experience. His enthusiasm enkindled and his creativity given direction, he went on to create a band of brothers who lived simply and in solidarity with the poor. Francis took his direction in life from this inner navigation (following his deepest enthusiasm wherever it led him) and created a new way of living and working with others. His enthusiasm was the key that opened up his inner life and creativity, and then joined that life to the service of his community.

Due to the split in our religious sensibility that has plagued us for centuries, we tend to experience our spiritual traditions turned upside down. In our religions there has long been a tendency to discount our own living, our experiences and our inner searching and questioning in favor of a top-down system of formation, direction, and organization. Ordinarily we were offered scripture, ready-made and digested theology together, with the lives of heroic individuals who lived in the past as models to emulate, and then given a creed of beliefs to commit to memory. Thus armed, we were expected to venture forth "into the world" to do the best we could to cope with its slings and arrows, to meet the hard challenges of living by copying the behavior of spiritual heroes or heroines. Frequently the mere possession of this body of creed and knowledge was offered to us as our "passport" to salvation.

The suggestion that we might be able to directly experience the presence of divine mystery in the midst of our lives, both in our enthusiasms and struggles, that in fact our daily living is the central arena where the encounter with the divine (spirituality) takes place, these notions were available only to a chosen few, usually those who chose religious life or ministry as a vocation. We were, in effect, cut off from our most fundamental spiritual nourishment and from the mystical experience that is at the roots of all religion. In Christianity, for example, surely the New Testament accounts of Jesus' birth are telling us, among other things, that the Great Mystery does not visit only the elite, that the divine is found in the most unexpected and unlikely places.

Thomas Berry points out that the primary revelation of God to us humans is not found in the scriptures, but in the natural world around us, in the book of creation. Somehow we got that turned around in the last few centuries. Now we find ourselves at the brink of irreversible destruction of the planet, so out of necessity we must re-examine our assumptions. The same wrong-end-around dynamic seems to operate for our own spiritual formation. What would our lives, our loves, and our vitality be like if we honored our own experiences and life-events as the first and primary source of divine self-communication to us?

In the Catholic tradition Father Andrew Greeley has pointed out that the sacraments — those bulwarks of the liturgy — exist for the purpose of celebrating and hallowing the grace and spirit that have already entered our lives. We encounter the divine mystery primarily in our daily living. The sacraments are there to single out and validate those encounters with grace and mystery and enable the whole community to bless them. The sacrament of baptism, for example, celebrates the miracle and extraordinary gift of a birth that has already happened. The sacrament of marriage consecrates and validates in the eyes of the community a sacred union, a spirit-filled and graced relationship that has already developed between two people. The sacrament does not make holy the relationship; the relationship is *already* holy, because all of life is holy. Greeley calls this interaction between life and our worship "empirical liturgy." He suggests that it is having this dynamic wrong-way-round that causes our worship to be often so dull, bloodless, and uninspired.

The Judeo-Christian scripture is a record of one person after another listening to his or her own experience, deciding that experience was God's way to communicate, and then finding validation, counsel, and support in their spiritual traditions. This is what happened to Moses, Abraham, Jeremiah, Ezekiel, and others in the Old Testament. In the New Testament Paul took his own life to the radical gospel message of Jesus and wove together a whole new theology for early Christianity. Francis of Assisi resonated inside when he heard a passage from the gospels that confirmed his heart's desire, that supported key movements of his life that he had experienced over and over again.

All of these figures in our religious past began with their own life experiences and then took their encounters with grace and divine mystery to the community and the tradition for critique and support. There is always the possibility that we can take wrong turns or travel down to dead ends in our interpretation of our life experiences. We need our spiritual traditions for guidance and help, but we also need to listen carefully to our own living.

Has this sacred and holy give-and-take process ceased to be valid in the last few centuries? Did it vanish along with some golden age of spiritual giants now long past?

What is the concrete result of this topsy-turvy in our religions and spiritualities? I suggest that we pay a very stiff price in our lives. We neglect and fail to honor or listen to our insides, our experiences, the diverse and fecund elements of our daily life. We do not feel that our inner being is a place that can be touched by the sacred. We are so poorly connected with our inner depths and alienated from our lives to such an extent now, it seems, that we are reluctant even to age, to mature, to grow old. We are mightily fearful of the death that is as much a part of our life as the birth that launched it. A trip to any greeting card store will reveal the disdain of aging that lives and seethes in our culture. Card after card on the racks heaps a kind of contempt on the very natural process of aging past forty, of maturing, of ripening. The recent hospice movement has brought attention to our culture's huge fear of death and our neglect and abandonment of the dying. Because that altar deep within us is barren of candles and flowers, because of this neglect of the sanctification of our own being, we deny life itself and allow our dying to become for us the ultimate boogey-man, instead of the natural transition it really is. When we see our lives and life experiences as so bereft of connection with the sacred, and thereby so untrustworthy, then surely it follows that our aging and dying will seem even more unreliable and God-forsaken. Henry David Thoreau, a famous simple-living adherent, wrote in his journal, "I will be happy to lie down in the ground for eternity, because I have so thoroughly loved that same earth in my life." Thoreau was a man who had not neglected those inner connections with the sacred, his spirituality.

What's Inside the Box?

Attention to our experiences and our inner life is vital to us also because our inner life opens us to a knowledge of who we are beyond our roles. Our society is plagued by epidemics of low self-esteem or self-esteem that is anemic because it's overly tied into our occupations and professions. Who are we beyond these roles? Only rich and deep connections with our inner life can give us the answers to these questions. Only the energetic crafting of a soul can enlarge our identity and give it significance by connecting it with all of creation.

Psychologist Dan Montgomery, author of *How to Survive Practically Anything,* describes a technique he uses with his clients in psychotherapy that often opens up for them the creativity and adventure of exploring the inner life. Montgomery asks his clients to construct an "art box." One selects a box of any size or shape to symbolize one's whole person — a shoe box, a hat box, whatever seems right. Then Montgomery has his client collect pictures, photos, images cut from magazines, drawings, words, poems, or objects that represent different aspects of that person's life. The outside of the box represents the "public self" — the outer shell one shows to the world. Inside the box, Montgomery encourages the client to select and place images that represent the inner self — one's dreams, feelings, secrets, desires, and most intimate experiences and yearnings and creative urges. Clients wind up constructing interesting and colorful collages both on the outside and inside of the box.

Montgomery describes one of his male clients who brought him a box richly decorated on the outside, but bare and empty on the inside. Decoration of the box became a real catalyst for that man, which opened him to considerable growth and development in his life as he searched for colorful and expressive images with which to decorate the inside. As he gained an intimacy with his inner world, the box began to fill with balloons and fantastic pictures.

A way I have found to get immediately in touch with my own inner life is to sit down and make a list of the people in the world (both living and deceased) I currently most admire, look up to, wish to emulate in my own living. Who are my mentors and teachers? Whose lives and examples stir my blood? I believe it was C. G. Jung who wrote that the qualities we most admire in others, especially in figures who are a bit larger than life (those who are heroes and heroines for us), catch our imagination in a vivid way because they mirror qualities that exist within our own hearts – those traits and virtues we most value and want to develop and bring to life creatively inside us and in our own living.

Try making such a list; it will reveal a lot to you. Here are some names from my most recent list: artist Grandma Moses; E. F. Schumacher, economist and author of *Small Is Beautiful: Economics As If People Mattered;* Edward Abbey, author of *The Monkey-Wrench Gang;* preacher and Franciscan priest Richard Rohr; illustrator Maurice Sendak; singer Van Morrison; artists Pablo Picasso and Henri Matisse; all the people who volunteer at school crossings each day; creation-spirituality guru Matthew Fox; America's national treasure, Henry David Thoreau; wicca-adherent and author Starhawk; geologian Thomas Berry; documentary filmmaker Michael Moore, who directed the film *Roger & Me;* Green activist Petra Kelly; musicians Miles Davis and Professor Longhair; Catholic Worker founder Dorothy Day... the list goes on and on. My roster of the admired tells me a lot about my own inner landscape — qualities that are most important to me (such as creativity, humor, outreach to others, commitment to healing the planet) — how I would like to be, what I aspire to. Make up a list of your own and see what you find out about your own innards.

Our inner life and experience are more trustworthy and reliable than we can imagine. Our friendships, our relationships, our struggles at work, our dreams, our enthusiasms, our inner conversations supply all that we need to flourish and grow and become better. A person with a strong inner life is often dismissed in our culture as a dreamer or "airhead." Yet just consider that the two greatest advances in twentieth-century science, relativity and quantum theory, were both arrived at intuitively, imaginatively — even in daydreams. It is reported that Niels Bohr, the father of quantum physics, came to his conception of electron behavior after dreaming one night about skating rinks. Albert Einstein stumbled on key components of relativity daydreaming about riding sunbeams. What a pair of space cadets! Yet see what lots of good stuff inside the box can do!

Joseph Campbell wrote extensively of the hero's journey in world mythology. Quite simply, the hero's journey is a call to embody our spirituality in our living, to make our inner life flesh and blood. "The soul's high adventure" (Campbell's phrase), this inner journey is an ongoing experience of one's own individuality, one's special uniqueness.

The Great Balancing Act

How do we live out our unique vision and embrace our own mystery? One way is to open the ancient overflowing tool box of our spiritual traditions. Nestled therein are many reliable implements that have stood the test of centuries of use in the work of creative inner integration and soul crafting. What are some of these ancient tools? Patience, silence, incubating darkness, the wonderful yeasting action of prayer, wise and careful discernment, the adventure of striving for simplicity, meditation techniques, the great and not-so-easy art of letting go, the simple craft of mindfulness, the call to the death-rebirth dynamic of the cocoon, the cultivation of a contemplative attitude, renunciation, fasting, attentiveness, and the endless mystery of forgiving others.

Once we have these tools at hand, where can they be put to work? Where else but in our everyday life? We do not naturally connect spiritual exercise with daily life. We identify the practice of spirituality with white flowing robes and far-off places – a monastery, a retreat center, or a misty landscape somewhere, empty of the humdrum and everyday. We wait for bewitching music, swelling cascades of violins like we hear in the movies, to cue us that this is a sacred moment. We over-romanticize spirituality, push it out of reach, waiting for just the right moment and occasion. We tell ourselves that it can't happen here – right in the living room with the kids and the TV on, or in the office with the boss hovering over my shoulder and spreadsheets sprawled across my desk.

Nevertheless it is our ordinary life that is the matter we are to transform into wholeness. It is an exhilarating truth that every moment of our daily life, every experience, at whatever time or place, can serve as spiritual exercise. The realm of the sacred is everywhere.

A few years ago my teenage stepson wanted a car. His request for help put me into a very uncomfortable, ambivalent place. Though convinced excessive driving is environmentally destructive, though I'd just written an article praising the virtues of environmental responsibility, I could also see that boredom and immobility would have been corrosive to his spirit at that important time in his life. Further, he needed some breaks in a life filled with mishaps and trials; he'd worked hard in school and was willing to work for the car's upkeep. I decided to give him a loan. Though I'd like to report that this deliberation proceeded with great-souled equanimity and grace on my part, alas, that was not the case. Kicking and screaming all the way, I found myself dragged through a dilemma that in the end resolved itself and resulted in real growth for me. The problem cornered me and forced me to let go of my own pet agendas and open myself to a wider vision and wisdom.

It was the late great Dr. Seuss himself who said, "Life is the Great Balancing Act!" Sorting through these difficult dilemmas, working out the necessary compromises, and finding practical workable solutions to knotty, seemingly unsolvable problems, I'm convinced, is true prayer, close encounters with divine mystery working in our lives. It is the painful arena of upset plans, nagging selfishness, tricky challenges, slippery banana peels under the feet of our easy posturing, the arena of self-emptying and surrender, where we are at once most human and most in touch with the divine. This is sacred work. Sometimes we must hold two equally balanced and strenuous tensions within us at the same time. When this happens – hard as it is to maintain – it is a very holy moment.

The ongoing effort to live simply and generously is rife with these kinds of balancing efforts and opportunities for soul growth. The spiritual discipline of discernment and the ancient virtue of prudence both stand us in good stead as we make choices and arrange our priorities.

We spend a great deal of our time in the workplace. Work, of course, has its many ups and downs – dealing with difficult people, striving hard not to be a difficult person in turn, negotiating the reefs, currents, and undertows that often impede getting the work done. In fact, our jobs can be as arduous, harrowing, fraught with danger and hardship, and as challenging and triumphant as any hero's journey described in adventure literature or classical epics. Sometimes we drop into our easy chair at home of an evening as travel-weary and wrung-out as any Odysseus home from ten years of wandering the wine-dark Aegean sea. In our own right, we have eluded siren-like voices, dodged the lotus-eaters, tricked the cyclops, navigated past whirlpools and clashing rocks, entered the cave of winds, and done heroic battle with overwhelming obstacles. Wily as serpents and innocent as doves we go out the door every morning. The workplace is as good a school for spirituality as any monastery. Our work, our homes, our neighborhoods, our public meeting places, our voting booths, our classrooms, our sidewalks – all are as conducive to the practice of spirituality as any ashram or retreat house. Our turf, our stuff, however cluttered and discombobulated, are holy ground. The ordinary hassles of daily living are rich soil in which to grow and bloom.

How does this spirituality of everyday life connect us with attempts to live simply? Because lifestyles are outward manifestations of inner reality, of a spiritual condition, it follows that our effort to live simply and generously can succeed only to the extent that we have built bridges between our daily living and a strong and rich inner life, an active spirituality. Simple living is also a way to strip the clutter from our lives so that we can make good use of the rich fertility our daily living offers for spiritual growth. Simplicity is part of the business of crafting a soul.

We must have access in equal measures to the wealth of our spiritual traditions, to the authentic and mysterious depths of our own selfhood and enthusiasms, to the riches of creation and to the sensibility of faith (trust that creation is blessing). These are the elements that make up a vital and vibrant spirituality for simple living. It is a worldly and ecological spirituality that says "yes" to life's riches, both inner and outer.

Ecology and Sanity

Spirituality is healthy. Many psychologists and others in the health professions have recognized the vital contribution spirituality makes to mental and physical well-being. Fran Ferder, a Catholic sister with a long and active practice in psychotherapy, points out that the Genesis accounts in the Bible describe God as Energizer, Breath-Sharer, one who hovers, who breathes life into and who wants to relate to all of creation. These same qualities, Ferder notes, also describe people who are psychologically healthy and robust. Such people behave in ways that give life to others. They attend to and want to relate with others in productive and meaningful ways. "When our lives most reflect the sacred pattern that brought us into being," Ferder writes, "perhaps then we are closest to the holy, and therefore the most whole and healthy." The longing for holiness and wholeness is also good mental hygiene, she concludes. Good spirituality is also good mental health.

Just recently we have even seen the emergence of an *ecological* concept of human health and sanity — eco-psychology or re-earthing or shamanic counseling, it is variously called. Eco-psychology asks this question: Is it possible to be a healthy and sane human while living on a sick and dying planet? An impetus for this linking together of ecology and environmentalism with psychology and mental health has been the popularity of the controversial Gaia hypothesis. Developed by British biochemist James Lovelock and American biologist Lynn Margulis in the 1970s, this theory proposes that the earth's life support systems, the biomass, play an *active, intelligent* role in preserving the conditions that guarantee the survival of life on earth. "On earth the environment has been made and monitored by life," writes Margulis, "as much as life has been made and influenced by the environment." This theory proposes that the biomass, in its long-term self-regulation, exhibits "the behavior of a single organism, even a living creature." The ancient Greek name "Gaia," for the earth goddess, has been attached to this concept of a living biomass.

The image of Gaia, the earth alive, captivates and enchants the imagination in a dramatic portrayal of ecological interdependence. Indeed, much of twentieth-century science supports and extends this finding of interdependence — that the cosmos is not an inert hierarchy but instead is a great web of interconnectedness. Our scientific view of the cosmos now pictures the universe as an epochs-old evolving partnership of physical and biological systems, reaching from our present human condition back 15 billion years to the birth of the universe, shrouded in mystery, the Big Bang. "We have life and mind as fully at home in the universe as any of the countless physical systems from which they

evolve," writes Theodore Roszak. "More hypotheti-
cally, we have the possibility that the self-regulating
biosphere continues to 'speak' through the human
consciousness, making its voice heard even within
the framework of modern urban culture."

This suggests that there is a direct, necessary, and
intricate link between each one of our human lives
and the life of the planet Earth, a notion that brings
us back to the vision quest of the Native American
spiritual traditions and to Joseph Campbell's advice
to follow our bliss. Campbell noted that when people
follow their enthusiasms and loves through life, there
is a commonly reported sense of being helped by
hidden hands. "Don't be afraid," Campbell advises,
"and doors will open where you didn't know they
were going to be. When you follow your bliss, you
put yourself on a kind of hidden track that has been
there all the time, waiting for you, and the life you
ought to be living is the one you are living."

So it is in this way that the road of soul-crafting
becomes the adventure of a lifetime. And it is an
adventure, the new discipline of eco-psychology suggests, precisely because our unique individuality, our
souls, exist in a wider living context — that of the
earth and the whole universe. We need to see the
needs of the planet and the needs of the person
placed on the same continuum. Each of us is in communion with the rest of creation, with all of its travail
and splendor. It is creation itself that provides those
helping hands.

Carl Jung called the ancient task of soul-making

"individuation." We incarnate our inner depths in our personality and in our day-to-day living. It is as though, when we are born, the universe asks a particular question. We answer that question in and through our life history, our unfolding story. Answering that question is the hero's journey. In living out our lives vigorously and with integrity and depth we take a whole new body of possibilities into the field of interpreted experience for the benefit of others, for the benefit of the earth — and even apparently for the benefit of the heavens.

Some of the most astounding and exhilarating discoveries made in recent years in the modern sciences of physics and cosmology are those that inform us about the direct connection between our living consciousness and the realm of stars and galaxies stretching off billions of light years into the far reaches of the universe. One literally cannot exist, it seems, without the other; each is the matrix and background for the other. Observations at the subatomic level, for example, clearly demonstrate this mysterious connection between consciousness and physical reality. Which facet of the wave-particle duality of matter that is manifested in a scientific observation depends entirely on the sort of question that is being asked by the observer. In a very real sense the observer creates the reality being observed.

In a fundamental way our souls and the universe are in cahoots. We adventure through our lives linked with vast alliances.

In the past two decades the science shelves in libraries and bookstores have featured works with deeply intriguing titles, such as *The Tao of Physics, The Dancing Wu Li Masters, In Search of Schrodinger's Cat,* or *God and the New Physics.* These books attempt to communicate to the lay person something of the wonder and sense of the marvelous that attends these connections science has stumbled upon in recent years. "Of all people today," writes physicist Alan Lightman, "I think scientists have the deepest faith in the unseen world. The greater the scientist, the deeper the faith." Not so very long ago scientists were the most hard-headed rationalists, leery of anything that smacked of the spiritual or mystical. How this turn-around has come about is directly related to discoveries that have been made in the last hundred years in the hardest science of them all – physics. A whole new background for the relationship between scientific research and religious questioning about how our human lives fit into the larger picture has been created.

Physics asks questions and then probes and observes in order to understand why things in nature are the way they are. The accumulated body of knowledge in modern physics suggests now that the reality that underlies our existence is nothing less than a riddle wrapped in an enigma stuck into the heart of a great puzzle. Infinitesimal particles pop into existence out of sheer nothingness then vanish back into the never-never land of quantum uncertainty. Speculation about the reality that underlies this kind of behavior of basic universal matter sounds outrageous, paradoxical, mind-blowing. Niels Bohr, the father of quantum physics, remarked once that if one is not thoroughly shocked by these revelations of modern physics, then one has not completely understood them.

Apparently the universe we inhabit is thoroughly and devotedly interrelated. Its underlying reality is dynamic and completely beyond conceptualization. Our universe is process. It is a web, a community, a vast interlocking fabric of relationships. Hildegard of Bingen, a medieval mystic who lived eight hundred years ago, described it this way: "Everything that is in the heavens, on the earth, or under the earth is penetrated with connectedness, full of relatedness." Some physicists now maintain that the whole universe is dynamically implied and, in a sense, hidden, contained, or enfolded into any of its parts, in what is called an "implicate order." The universe is a completely undivided and seamless whole — even the "objective" observer cannot be separated out from it.

Awe and wonder in the face of the huge mysteries of our existence stir our spiritualities to life. Each and every one of us lives out our unique lives, and this living is an essential and necessary part of the weave of the fabric that is the universe. We look around us and see much cause for despair, but also much cause for hope, as our living takes on ever deeper levels of meaning. "New vistas of unspeakable wonder are opening up before us," writes physicist Michael Talbot. "Humankind is on the verge of the incredible."

Chapter 4

In Praise of Reading

ONE OF THE GOLDEN MEMORIES from my childhood is of long-ago trips to the library. My parents began to take me when I was seven or eight. Friday evenings were usually reserved for these visits. The books were catalogued, numbered, and tucked away on shelves in an old stone and tile-roofed house that sat flanked by rows of tall elms and sycamores at one corner of a major intersection in the city.

Inside were four floors, room after fabulous room crammed from scuffed wooden floors to high decorated ceilings with books of every sort and description. The interior of the library was complicated with passageways, arched hallways, nooks and crannies, narrow staircases winding up into darkness. Tall windows with dusty marble sills framed views of the streetlights and shadowed sidewalks outside, of leaves trembling in the night breezes. Within each room squatted heavy oak tables, their varnished surfaces gleaming in mellow pools of lamp glow. Only the slow ticking of a clock, some faraway murmurs, and an occasional footfall on the stairs disturbed the hush and whispering calm of the place.

After entering one of the rooms and tugging on the light string I would circumnavigate the walls, slowly browsing, pulling a book from its place in the stacks, reading a few sentences, looking at the pictures, and then slipping it back into its place in the row. Along one wall towered tall cliffs and wide battlements of science books and histories. Neat ranks of nature books, bird guides, and how-to manuals frowned down over dusty shelves packed with biographies, their Dewey decimal numbers carefully inked on the spines. English and American literature loomed, high and forbidding, on the opposite wall.

Nestled back in a shadowy corner upstairs was a large collection of children's books leaning against one another at odd angles on the shelves. In an alcove nearby were science fiction volumes in textured bindings. The titles of these books, eye-openers like *The War of the Worlds, The Martian Chronicles, The Stars My Destination,* tantalized me maddeningly, irresistibly. Mysteries and ghost stories lurked within a bay window on the top floor. Some of my favorites brooded in the gloom up there: *The Phantom Rickshaw, The Clue in the Embers, The Twisted Claw.*

Upstairs and down I would make my rounds. Dazzled by the wealth around me, I prowled amid fairy tales, myths, epics, adventure stories, sagas of exotic travel, catalogs of information, picture books, novels. My pile got higher and higher until finally the limit was reached. Then, after the librarian (the wonder-vendor) had checked me out, back into the dark outside I would go, arms laden with a fresh supply of reading, touched by the glory of books. Once home I would be lost for the rest of the evening off in the other worlds or deep within the one I already knew.

Robinson Crusoe surprised by a lone footprint on the beach. Tom Sawyer lost in the cave with Becky Thatcher. Holmes and Watson afoot on the Baskerville moors. Frodo the Hobbit in the land of Mordor. Pippi Longstocking in the south seas. Mowgli stalking the fearsome tiger, Shere Khan, with Bagheera the panther at his side. The cat in the hat. The pit and the pendulum. The call of the wild. The pursuit of the White Whale. Sighting Treasure Island off the bow of the *Hispaniola*. All of us who were ever rebuked as children for always having our noses in a book have been to these places, known these unforgettable characters, shared in these larger-than-life experiences. These images from the world's treasure of imaginative literature have long since passed from the page and into our hearts.

The passion for reading is one of the great gifts. If spirituality is all about recognizing and discovering, valuing and honoring the true pleasures of life, then reading good books, I believe, takes an important place in this quest for a fuller, more fulfilled existence. The satisfactions of reading are rich, deep, and permanent. Books reveal life to us in all its splendor, sadness, and complexity. Reading them can be a major help toward wholeness.

Reading quality books predisposes us for the adventure of contemplative living. Time spent between the covers of the world's great imaginative literature gets us into the habit of looking under the surface of things. Our ability to make connections, to realize insights into what joins us together as humans, is developed, exercised, and nurtured more and more as we read. The enjoyment of fine literature stimulates us to begin and to continue that dialogue with the world and with our own best self that makes up a rich inner life. Reading adds great depth to our own individual experiences.

There is a life-giving quality in the encounter between a reader and a lively book. When the nose is deep within their pages faith in the delight and beauty of the world is alive and flourishing. Quality books celebrate human relationships, the joys and even the trials of living, the wonders of the world. "By the poet's grace we have become the pure and simple subject of the verb 'to marvel,' wrote the French philosopher Gaston Bachelard. He called good books "reserves of enthusiasm."

There is a quality of magic alive in the reader's mind. Watching television, our national pastime, is inadequate to stir it. TV shows us too much. The magic never has a chance to work. We become passive-aggressive. Books, on the other hand, make demands on our curiosity, our ability to imagine, our sympathy, our sense of humor, our own inner artistry. When we can rise to these challenges the rewards are great because reading is an activity in which we *actively* participate. "The beholder," Oscar Wilde wrote, "lends to the beautiful thing its myriad meanings and makes it marvelous." The genuine artistry in us that is stimulated in reading expresses itself in the way we read and in the way we live.

Masterpieces of the imagination contain within them dangerous visions. They are exhilarating, eccentric, troublesome, and continually surprising. They can upset our worldview, restore us to our sense. They usually have a way of persuading us to ally ourselves with what is right, to sympathize with the good and the true and to disdain and scorn what is wrong, what is cowardly, what is not genuine, what is lacking in integrity. In the matter of developing values books are invaluable aids. They have influence.

Besides being lessons in the art of living great works of the imagination are a kind of vaccination against bigotry and intolerance. A well-crafted book has the ability to convey to us what it's like to be someone else. We can assume the very fiber and being of another's life. We can know something of the thoughts, the sound, the fury, the quiet, the varied emotions and sensuousness of another's existence. Perhaps then readers are less likely to respond with hatred and suspicion to someone who dresses, acts, thinks, and lives in a different way. Readers are used to getting inside another's skin. A reader's reaction is more likely to be interest in why that person dresses that way, in how that person thinks, and in the details of how that person lives.

In short, reading can enlarge and expand our interiors and keep our minds busy and far away from pettiness.

What should we read? Traffic in what you enjoy by all means, but once in a while try one of the classics, one of those magnificent works of the human imagination that are reprinted over and over down the years. Conveyors of wisdom and wonder, they are usually also bottomless wells of delight, real entertainments. Between their covers is a vast knowledge of and insight into the human heart together with truths we can feel deep in our bones.

Take, for example, Mark Twain's masterpiece, *The Adventures of Huckleberry Finn*. Twain wrote that his novel was a hymn set down in prose to give it a more worldly air. Besides being a wonderfully entertaining tale of a boy's odyssey down the Mississippi River, the book is also an illumination, a wise vision with a depth and mysteriousness that adds greatly to its appeal. A few pages into the story and we realize we are in the middle of a masterfully interwoven texture of character and event. Taken as a whole the book *is* like a hymn – a celebration of the comedy and tragedy of life and of the natural world. It easily infects us with its reserves of enthusiasm.

No one fails so pitifully to live up to the expectations of respectable society as Huck Finn. Yet there beats within him a heart filled with compassion.

Huck sends help back to two would-be murderers who are stranded on a wrecked steamboat. He feels pity for two swindlers who have been caught and punished by an outraged townspeople. His love for his companion on the river, Jim, knows no bounds.

And, leavened no doubt by a good mixture of solitude and society, Huck has learned in his life to look for beauty, to notice the world around him and to appreciate it deeply. Listen to him describe a summer thunderstorm over the river:

> It would get so dark that it looked all blue-back outside, and lovely; and the rain would thrash along by so thick that the trees off a little ways looked dim and spider-webby; and here would come a blast of wind that would bend the trees down and turn up the pale underside of the leaves; and then a perfect ripper of a gust would follow along and set the branches to tossing their arms as if they were just wild; and next, when it was just about the bluest and blackest — fst! It was bright as glory, and you would have a little glimpse of treetops a-plunging about away off yonder in the storm, dark as sin again in a second, and now you'd hear the thunder let go with an awful crash, and then go rumbling, grumbling, tumbling down the sky toward the underside of the world, like rolling empty barrels downstairs.

Someone once described contemplation as a love affair with reality. One eye out for the beauty, power and solace of the river he cherishes, the other eye on the foibles, sorrows, and humor in the circumstances of human life wherever it is found, Huck Finn is one of the great lovers, a model contemplative in many ways. This wonderful book is the harvest of those two eyes.

Books can take us to important places. The ultimate origin of religion lies in those experiences in which the divine breaks through and transfigures ordinary events with a sense of the sacred, moments that are touched by the Holy and visited with awe. One of the finest descriptions of such a moment occurs in the pages of the timeless children's classic, *The Wind in the Willows,* by Kenneth Grahame.

Mole and Rat, two of the animal characters in the book, are searching in a rowboat for a companion who is lost in the river country where they make their home. Rat suddenly sits up in the stern of the boat and begins to listen intently to something far off in the distance. He sinks back in his seat after a moment with a sigh and says:

> "So beautiful and strange and new! Since it was to end so soon, I almost wish I had never heard it. For it has roused a longing in me that is pain, and nothing seems worthwhile now but just to hear that sound once more and go on listening to it forever."

He hears it again. He is silent for a long while, completely spellbound. Finally, he exclaims,

"O Mole! The beauty of it! The merry bubble and joy, the thin, clear, happy call of the distant piping! Such music I never dreamed of, and the call in it is stronger even than the music is sweet! Row on, Mole, row! For the music and the call must be for us."

"I hear nothing myself," Mole admits. Rat doesn't answer. He is possessed in all his being by this new thing. Finally Mole begins to hear the music also. Tears come to both their eyes. Following the summons of this unearthly music they row on. They come to a small island in the river. The two moor their little boat on the margin of the island and go ashore.

Then suddenly the Mole felt a great Awe fall upon him, an awe that turned his muscles to water, bowed his head, and rooted his feet to the ground. It was no panic terror — indeed he felt wonderfully at peace and happy — and it was an awe that smote and held him and, without seeing, he knew it could only mean that some august Presence was very, very near. With difficulty he turned to look for his friend, and saw him at his side cowed, stricken, and trembling violently. And still there was utter silence in the populous bird-haunted branches around them.

The best children's books especially can put us directly in touch with that simple awe that not only holds us in thrall as we read but also enables us to share in what has been the impetus throughout human history for shaping and building great cathedrals, for composing magnificent symphonies, for constructing radio telescopes and rockets to the moon, for falling down on our knees in worship and praise. Awe and wonder are the most healing and energizing of emotions.

When life has become too complicated, when things are just too much, go borrow a good book from the nearest child. Or, better, revive that fine old custom of sitting down of an evening to read to children. Know for a short time once again the astonishment of being. "Childhood is not something which dies within us and dries up as soon as it has completed its cycle," another philosopher has said. "It is not a memory. It is the most living of treasures and it continues to enrich us without our knowing it." Adults need to curl up to a good tale as much as any child. Good reading can foster and restore in us and in our children a hope-filled approach to living. The encounter of one imagination with another can "purge from our inward sight," says the poet Shelley, "the film of familiarity which obscures from us the wonder of our being." Good books remind us of the riches we already possess; the ability to see beauty anywhere, the capacity for awe and for compassion, for taking joy and delight in the simplest things.

Early in *The Wind in the Willows* Mole emerges from his underground life and ventures forth into the wide world. Right away he discovers the river. Never in his life had he seen one before. Meandering aimlessly along its banks he is bewitched, entranced, enchanted completely by his new thing. Grahame writes here a fitting tribute to all imaginative literature:

> By the side of the river he trotted as one trots, when very small, by the side of a man who holds one spellbound by exciting stories; and when tired at last, he sat on the bank, while the river chattered on to him, a babbling procession of the best stories in the world, sent from the heart of the earth to be told at last to the insatiable sea.

Essayist Lance Morrow recalls a difficult time in his life when he was recovering from major heart surgery. He got himself through the arduous convalescence and readjustment by plowing through Shelby Foote's three-volume history of the Civil War. A woman close to him, he recalls, lost her son by drowning the night of his high school graduation. She endured through the weeks and months after this tragic loss partly by reading and rereading the works of Willa Cather. The calm and clarity of Cather's prose stabilized the woman and helped her through the darkest days and nights.

Reading can keep us sane and full of heart. Good books put us in genuine touch with other imaginations and intelligences. They are inoculations against cynicism and despair. With a good book under our arm or perched on our nightstand at home, we can probably rest assured we'll always be ready and able to soak up grace and spirit wherever they are found.

Books aren't very expensive and give us a wonderfully large return on our investment.

Do you find yourself growing grim about the mouth? Is it a damp and drizzly November in your soul? Pick up a good book.

Chapter 5

In Praise of Walking

THE TIME HAS COME AGAIN to say a good word on behalf of walking. In a day when anyone can change from jogging shoes, drive easily to the nearest airport, there to be whisked by jumbo jet in a few hours to almost any corner of the earth, I want to sing the praises of hoofing it. With a caution first to always watch out for traffic, I urge you to now and then cover a mile or two by legwork alone. Let us quietly celebrate here the charms of the nearest footpath, the smug satisfactions of owning a well-scuffed pair of stout hiking boots, the seductions of daily putting a leash on the dog and stepping outside, the never-ending allure of the city's gleaming sidewalks.

To begin, walking is probably the perfect all-around exercise. There is a wealth of evidence from the specialists to support this claim. Physical fitness experts extol walking as the ideal activity for keeping the body in shape. Walking is an aerobic exercise. This means that a brisk walk increases both heart rate and overall oxygen consumption. A good stroll through the neighborhood also lowers high blood pressure, actively stimulates the digestive system, tones the leg muscles, and is an effective aid to sleep. There are also beneficial effects on posture, lower back alignment, and a reduction of serum cholesterol levels. Walking is excellent (and cheap) medicine.

Walking improves circulation in general throughout the body. It helps keeps the heart ticking away in good sound order. And a daily regimen of walking is an ideal way to help control weight. A vigorous walk of half an hour burns 180 to 250 calories. A walk like that every day means a weight loss of fifteen pounds a year – without any change in eating habits! Walking can be every bit as effective as jogging in keeping weight under control.

A natural tranquilizer, walking also helps you cope with stress. It is a tension-reliever. Anxiety drains away as your pace relaxes into a steady rhythm. The interaction of body with mind during a good walk around the park simply untangles many of the day's knots. A sense of well-being and of accomplishment results from a steady schedule of footslogging. It is the glory and grace of this simple exercise of walking that it permits us to take leave for a while from the manipulations and judgments of our daily lives. This can be a powerfully effective aid in fighting off depression and in the maintenance of a good emotional balance.

Walking is fairly easy. It is sensible. It is accessible to nearly everyone. It requires no special equipment, no expensive outlay for paraphernalia. Walking is as natural to the human body as breathing. The body itself was built for use and functions much better when all its parts regularly have a chance to work in harmony together.

In addition to these very impressive benefits to our physical and mental health, walking offers more. A kind of wonderful alchemy takes place during a long walk. Why does a person begin to pace back and forth when she is seeking a solution to a difficult problem? When you are stuck, unable to go either forward or backward, just spinning wheels, take a stroll around the block. A hike seems to heighten consciousness. You feel more creative, with an enlarged sense of possibilities. You don't even have to mull over the problem while you are out on the sidewalks. It's best when the problem is out of mind. Just think pleasant thoughts, enjoy the passing view, or worry about something else (no shortage of grist for that mill). Meanwhile, the problem at hand sinks slowly out of sight into the murky depths of the unconscious where it will roll and churn about, finally bubbling and floating to the top — along with maybe an unforeseen solution.

Hal Borland, a nature writer, suspects that it is possible to gauge a person's mental breadth and depth by examining his or her attitude toward walking. Does he like to walk? Where does she go for walks? How often? Why? Or does that person, when you show up a bit footweary on her doorstep, look at you in absolute horror and exclaim: "You mean you *walked?*"

Walkers are a kind of secret society. Those who go regularly afoot even have time as they pass to nod or to wave. I have noticed that it is impossible to encounter another person on a backpacking trail without at least saying hello. More often than not, long, easy conversations take place between complete strangers. By the time the heavy packs are once again shouldered, fast friends have been made.

Taking a walk is a friendly way to take the true measure of things. A sense of proportion and of perspective seems to return. We are able to get our feet back on the ground. Truth often comes to meet us in new ways. And a daily walk is a regular lesson in old-fashioned virtues like patience, steadfastness, and the almost priceless ability to be contentedly unhurried. Walkers are perhaps less likely than others to mortgage the present for some far-off future.

And walking is, among all these other salutary benefits, an almost complete introductory course in holistic spirituality. Walking is complex, involving mind and body, heart and soul — all working together, the very essence of good health. "I celebrate," wrote Robert Louis Stevenson, "that fine intoxication that comes of much motion in the open air, that begins in a sort of dazzle and sluggishness of the brain, and ends in a peace that passes all understanding. Your muscles are so agreeably slack, you feel so clean and strong and so idle, that whether you move or sit still, what you do is done with pride and a kingly sort of pleasure."

I am much addicted to walking in all its variety. In addition to the after-dinner stretch and the Sunday afternoon promenade in the park, there is also sauntering, scrambling, vagabonding, hiking, snowshoeing, pilgrimaging, and trekking. I am a special fan of the common nature walk. Others are inveterate city explorers. I have sampled those pleasures, but for me nothing can match a hike up hill or down vale, far from the clatter and noise and ringing telephones of town. I like to hang around footpaths and trails wearing old clothes and good sturdy shoes. Gurgling brooks, pine-scented air, and songful meadowlarks perched on fenceposts send me reeling off into ecstasy.

For me, an afternoon's walk down a woodland trail is often a helpful lesson in the fine art of contemplation. It doesn't always work. I am still a novice. But when things come together and I am able to cast off my careworn discontent and city-bred frantic hurry, when I can slow down and when things really click, then I am able to enter more deeply into a centering experience that pays dividends elsewhere in my life.

Attentive but relaxed, I walk just to hear the simple candor of the everyday, well lost and adrift on the meandering currents of an afternoon. If I am out just to discover, to see how spring or autumn is coming along, then a moment-by-moment waking up will ordinarily take place. The way the sunlight shines through the oak leaves overhead as they dance and flutter in the winds, the feel of breezes across my neck and face, the honeysuckle smells mingled with the damp earth aroma, the magic music of a wood thrush heard in the distance, the broad blue skies and clouds overhead – these are the cues that prompt the awakening. Called insistently beyond myself, I am invited to open my eyes wider and wider to the world.

If I am out to think something through or in a meditative frame of mind, then slowly my thoughts will grow and ripen like the blackberries on the bushes alongside the trail. For an instant maybe I feel as though I have realized something extremely important. Then it escapes me as quickly as it came. But it doesn't matter. As the hours and the miles slip by I am beginning to feel more and more at home in the universe. I really belong here. A kind of sturdy and durable hope begins to arise in me. I see shiny flecks of what may, further down the path, turn out to be tiny nuggets of real wisdom.

My senses all stimulated by the plain joy of walking, a quiet exuberance flows within. I am beginning – to some extent anyway – to feel in tune with the wide wavelengths of the here and now. And there is some very real centering going on within, the kind the spiritual directors and gurus talk about. My center of gravity is lowered. Interior shiftings and relocations are taking place. I am somehow restored to a sense of intimacy with my own inner life. The resources and strengths contained therein seem more accessible.

This experience of centering has its roots, I think in both the cultivation of simplicity that goes with walking and the wide-awake contemplative way in which we become intimate with the world and our own interiors. On a nature walk, my body feeling alive and good, my heart pierced by the beauty of the woodlands, I am emptied, ready for anything, and able for a few moments at least to look at things with wonder-seeing eyes. When I am walking, before the workaday world once again beckons, I feel myself to be an intrepid explorer, a tireless hunter of the real treasures of life. To locate these treasures we must be both simple and wise.

One unforgettable evening I took a walk up through an old pasture that I had visited a hundred times before. It was a favorite haunt. A summer thunderstorm had just passed through. Shreds, layers, and towering Himalayas of dark clouds, flashing with lightning, receded into the hazy distances. Tatters and wisps of fog rose ghostlike out of the soft evening folds of the nearby valleys. As the twilight began to deepen, scarlet patches of open sky appeared brilliant in the west among the dark sooty clouds.

Suddenly out of this shaggy field around me, which was so overgrown and crowded with summer wildflowers that it had become an ornate patchwork bouquet stretching from fence to fence, common fireflies – hundreds upon hundreds of them – came out of the wet grass and floated slowly over the colorful outbursts of daisies, sunflowers, and Queen Anne's lace still splattered with raindrops.

The firefly host looked like an immense fleet of tiny balloons made of pearly light. They were like wandering, flickering galaxies of stars honoring the earth with an unhurried visit. Hundreds of frogs joined their throaty trills with the loud praise-psalms of the whippoorwills. Mists veiled the far-off hillsides. Finally, the dusk dissolved into a velvet black. Only the numberless gliding and flashing lanterns of the fireflies were left to make a luminous darkness of the vast ocean of a midsummer night.

An evening's walk had brought me to a spellbound moment wherein beauty had gifted me lavishly. There is greatness, sublimity, divinity everywhere in the world, and it is worthy of worship and praise. It was a moment overflowing with grace. And one I still keep within me, wrapped and tucked away like a jewel. I can rely on it, I think, to help sustain me through hard times. There are many other such moments locked away in this treasure house, encounters with the common miracles of everyday: thunder in winter, moon-silvered shadows in a midnight forest, wild geese calling to one another as they fly northward overhead, sunrises in the mountains.

"If you would know the blessedness of a cheerful heart," John Burroughs, one of America's foremost nature writers, wrote a hundred years ago, "then invest in common things and be content with a steady and moderate return." To cultivate the habit of walking is, I believe, to make one of the very best investments possible. This modest practice can be a lifetime prescription for continued health and joyful living. And walking can be an invaluable aid in personal transformation, a discipline in learning to live a life of trust and simplicity, a help on the way to wholeness: that place where the love that moves the sun and the stars makes its nest snugly in the palm of your hand.

Ultimately, of course, we are called by this love to community and to commitment with others. We cannot spend all of our time blithely strolling through the woods and across the fields. Beauty alone is not enough. But on the long and difficult road to the reign of God I hope that I will always be among those who, once in a while, turn down the ride and go afoot.

Chapter 6

In Praise of Nature

I ONCE LIVED FOR A TIME in the Missouri Ozarks, the hill country in the southern part of the state. While staying down in Mad Dog Hollow, the valley where I built my house, I was haunted. The stones haunted me. Let me explain.

In spring and in autumn there is no more lovely place in the country than the Ozark mountains. On a fine day in April stand on a ridgetop there and look out over the hills and valleys stretching off into the distance. Genuine beauty, you will see, is a commonplace here, part and parcel of the place. The soft shades of green hillsides are punctuated by white puffs of flowering dogwood and patches of blooming redbud. Down in the hollows rushing waters trip and tumble over falls and then pause in deep, clear eddies before flowing calmly out over pebbled watercourses shaded by scented thickets of spicebush and beech. Two dozen different kinds of songbirds sing to the hills from dawn until dusk.

Six months later, October stops you dead in your tracks. Mouth agape, you are dazzled by the color-splashed hillsides. Flocks of migrating birds call as they circle the unshorn pastures bordered with fiery red sumacs and mottled orange sassafras. Harvest smells awaken rich and nameless yearnings from rootless spirits within. The sparkling air intoxicates like a good wine. When you have to go back indoors, you feel torn away, bereft, needlessly absent from a not-to-be-missed festival.

But when winter, that old Puritan come down from the north, arrives and unpacks his frosty bags, then it is a very different thing.

Autumn colors long faded into tattered rags, cold fronts pounce on Mad Dog Hollow like beasts of prey. With day after day starved of sunlight, gray clouds stretching from horizon to horizon, with long sieges of darkness and always the frost and cold that strip the land of leaf and color, this time could be very drab and monotonous in the Ozarks. An afternoon in mid-January would sometimes put me in closer touch with my own worst demons than I ever care to be again. But I learned more in the end from this stark season than I did from any of the others.

Cabin fever would often drive me outdoors to walk the hillsides. The lush green cover of summer was only a memory like a calendar page tucked back behind the others. The oaks and hickories stood in stripped ranks on the hillsides. The architecture of the place was in plain view. On these walks I learned that these cold months had their own quiet beauty and offered unique pleasures and satisfactions. Winter made everything honest and straightforward. The cold season revealed what would go unnoticed other times of the year. I'm talking about the stones of Mad Dog Hollow.

The Stone on My Shelf

The Ozark landscape — wherever it isn't a stream or a river — is constructed of good reliable rock. From the huge boulders on the ridges, through the field stones underfoot, to the flinty streambed gravel, stone is everywhere. If Detroit one day invented an auto engine that ran on crushed rocks, every Ozarker would outshine the wealthiest Persian Gulf sheik. Wherever this plentiful rock presents an exposed surface to the open skies and winds, nature takes the opportunity to decorate the stones as surely as some New Yorkers do their subway cars. In the Big Apple they do it with spray paint. In the Ozarks nature decorates with lichens.

Lichens are pioneer plants that form large, colorful patches on tree bark or on exposed rock surfaces. They are tough and long-lived. These lichens crust, etch, and overlay stone and boulder with detailed figures and elaborate, fanciful designs. They form interweaved areas of delicate colors, wandering watercourse lines, overlapping shield-like circles, and curiously shaped discs. They are very beautiful.

In contrast to the winter landscape, patches of these humble plant forms cannot help but catch one's eye – like a drop of fresh blood on a newly fallen snowdrift. Once you notice them for the first time, maybe on a solitary December stroll, you begin to see them everywhere, especially after a soaking rain when their subtle earth colors glow with some kind of inner light.

Nature is whimsical with her immense talents. It is as though Michelangelo had painted his elaborate frescoes on the sidewalks and doorsteps of the Roman slums rather than on the vaulted and incensed ceilings of the Vatican chapels. These samples of nature's folk art lay strewn about everywhere in the hollows. They would never fail to astonish me anew when I ran across them on my winter walks. One day I picked up an especially fine specimen and carried it home with me. I placed the embellished stone on a shelf where I could keep an eye on it. Often a glimpse of it on that shelf would put me in touch with nameless pangs of longing arising from deep within. Associated with this stone was a nagging sense that I had lost something irreplaceable or a feeling of bittersweet nostalgia for I knew not what. Sharp arrows would stab at my heart, catching me unaware.

The stone haunted me. It sat up on its shelf like an icon, one of those religious paintings from the Eastern church. And, as an icon is intended to do, it represented a vast mysterious background that existed behind the adorned reality of its surface. I began to realize that the stone, for me, was an emblem. It stood for something. I had brought a piece of whatever it was indoors. And it insisted I pay attention. The stone on my shelf turned out to be a burning bush.

This icon gathering dust on my shelf, I came to understand, stood for all the wealth in nature that I had found on my walks – the generous and handsome felicity of the earth. It stood for the curious way in which a dogwood flower is shaped. It stood for the majestic and shifting shadowland shapes of everyday summer clouds. It was the startling surprise of a lightning bolt. It was the handsome charm of an emerging oak leaf in spring, the silhouette of a spreading white oak seen against the wintry charcoal-ash sky. It was the way a snowflake looks, the shockingly colorful designs on a butterfly's wings, moonlight's silver gleaming on icicles, cinnamon leaves coated delicately with frost, painted desert skies above a sunset tinted with fire and eggshell colors.

Make up for yourself a litany of nature's most ordinary and pleasing details like this. See how our daily bread is ever to be touched by the grace of the commonplace.

The gift of beauty from the earth's heart was represented in the stone. The stone conjured up for me all the awe and wonder gleaned from years of intimate encounter with the natural world in the Ozarks, those times when I was able to make close acquaintance with the seasons in their moods, the winds in their different tempers, the trees, waters, and mists, shades and silences, and all the varied voices of inanimate things. A moment's glance at the shelf summoned all kinds of good memories, packed and stored away within.

There was a morning once when I crouched on a high bluff overlooking an Ozark river and watched the elegant takeoff of a blue heron up through the mists that entwined the tops of the sycamore trees. Or a late evening in May when, below arches and domes of stormy clouds, I waded across a field up to my waist in wildflowers while bluebirds warbled from the branches of a nearby apple tree and two owls called to each other down in the shades of the hollow. And there was a clear March night when I lay on a hilltop and, with powerful binoculars, looked straight up into the unimaginable suburbs of the Milky Way, that vast banner of worlds far away and flung in remotest splendor across the black enamel of the night sky.

Memorable and awestruck moments like these accumulate in a lifetime. They add up to something. There are secret places within us that are stirred deeply and passionately by them. The innards of our hearts reverberate with their endless echoes. They end up stored away in us for use as incantations against despair and darkness. "We can never have enough of nature," wrote Thoreau. "We must be refreshed by the sight of inexhaustible vigor." The stone sitting on my shelf bore the weight of immense glories — and much more.

The Trickster of Mad Dog Hollow

Even after I had arrived at this explanation, the stone on my shelf persisted in haunting me, insistently tugging at my sleeve like a questioning child. Taking that stone in my hand some nights when the paper-soft moths fluttered outside the window panes, I'd feel myself paused at the door of beckoning shadows and mystery. The stone marked a boundary beyond which existed something wholly other from me.

The haunting continued, and it took me much longer to get to the next level of explanation. But it was one of my near neighbors, the chat, who set me on the right path.

There's more to nature than just the calendar-photo picturesque. Acquaintance with the Ozarks, for example, soon revealed the place to be...well, eccentric and sometimes hard and problematic. Its tumbledown rivers, disheveled glades, and hump-shouldered hills were often visited by weather that was gloomy and morose. Plunging, thicketed ravines hid bristling lowland woods buried under phantasmal shawls of mist and fog. Winter could bring those black-hearted days, dark and still save for the bad-tempered cawings of crows. Late July offered chiggers, ticks, and humidity so heavy and thick you could lean back against it and be held up. Upland glades crowded with wildflowers were bordered with stunted and gnarled blackjack oaks that looked villainous and menacing.

None of this was what I had expected. A life-long

city dweller, when I moved to the country I planned to be always snug in the midst of pleasing landscapes like those pictured in the TV ads of some corporation trying to show how earth-friendly it is. But on some nights thunder prowled. Billows of cloud would part to reveal the rising moon, pale and bloodshot and spectral like some ghastly balloon ascending through the thorn-bristling brush and then lighting the Ozark forest with a wan and pearly light that would set the screech owls to cry out their desolate wails, what sounded to me like, "Oh, I wish I'd never been born!" Then I had to reconsider and revise both my expectations and the notion lodged in my head that creation was finished once and for all. "No, no!" shouted the brood of mother night, "Creation is here! And now!"

Nothing educated and informed me about the Ozarks' quirks and idiosyncrasies better than the chat, the trickster of Mad Dog Hollow. Through my open window of a spring morning came up-tempo and songful avian melodies all right, but also the odd talkathon of a secretive bird known as the chat, a kind of large warbler that frequented the wild plum groves near my house. The chat's normal voice sounded like a rusty old truck trying to start on a cold morning. The bird would get revved up and then, like a demented mockingbird, hurl out from the midst of the thicket a medley of grotesque squawks, robust whistles, hoarse curses, tinny catcalls, a rude noise or two followed by maniacal cackles and neurotic chatterings. It sounded like all hell breaking loose.

Now and then I invested in some stalking time

and would watch the fellow perched on a vine, jerking his tail up and down and delivering his animated briarpatch monologue. The bird would pause now and then to dive headfirst into a nearby tangle of leaves. It would reappear high in an adjacent pine tree and then fly off with its tail hanging straight down in a deranged sort of flight over to a tree stump. Landing awkwardly, it would posture for a moment, doing a Buster Keaton kind of routine, and then vanish completely from sight, but not from hearing. Finally the chat would stop in mid-cluck and from far off in the forest the shimmering lyrics of a summer tanager or the soft gentle warbling of a bluebird would restore something of bird song's lost reputation.

The Ozarks' moods and rock-strewn complexity would often throw me off balance. Expecting sweet melodies, I would get the chat's minstrel show. But in the end the place got under my skin and wholly charmed me in completely unanticipated ways like that half-cracked, outlandish uncle who turned up when we were kids, hiding unexpected gifts behind his back while he demonstrated the latest gimmick, trick, or joke from the novelty store. Uncle Brian came with joy buzzer in hand from a larger world than the one we daily inhabited. His visits compelled us to expand our worlds to make room for him and his chuckle-headed antics and stories.

I had come to the Ozarks for pretty pictures and received instead a much greater prize and revelation. Here the high-spirited energies of the earth had heaved up a shaggy, itchy, moonstruck wilderness — a place of blessing, extravagance, and roughshod beauty that could just break your heart sometimes, like the sight of a bluebird preening its celestial-colored feathers while perched on a knob-gnarled and cobwebby postoak branch.

The stone turned out to be an antenna that tuned me in to the wide wave-lengths that were the *wholeness* of this place. Rootless and exiled spirits within me, full of imagination and desires and curiosities, met an outmatchingly muscular and heartily large and promiscuous landscape without. Enduring connections were made between the smaller and larger geographies. The Ozark land was incomprehensibly rich and whole and beguiling. It required as its essential elements both the sweet songs of the tanager and bluebird together with the ravings and tomfoolery of the chat and the ill-tempered crows, both the beauty of the wildflower-bedecked hillsides and the wicked tangles of briar and poison-ivy in the ravines.

The wholeness here derived from the wildness here. Though the Ozarks had been stripped of its virgin timber a hundred years ago and widely settled, there were still scattered throughout the region large tracts of forest and glade empty of human habitation or interference. Stepping out the door of my house, I could walk due south for probably twenty miles or so before I came to a road or another house. There still survived enough untampered-with land and life that the cumulative result, though a mere pastiche of the untrammeled wilderness that once existed here, was a refuge and sanctuary for wildness in an overly tamed and domesticated country. My home was only a pale remnant of that vast deciduous forest John James Audubon once described as so continuous and pervasive that a squirrel could have crossed from the Atlantic shore to the Mississippi River without once touching the ground. But enough remained.

Once I was exploring a remote hollow I had never before visited. It was in early June, a stormy day. The somber pageantry of clouds hid the sun. Mists were forming up around the garrets and lofts of the ridge-crests. As I entered the deeper woods of the lower hollow, the sky darkened. Down the path an animal disappeared quickly in a blur of movement before I could get a good look. A rain crow's long labored call echoed against the stern hillside. A nuthatch circled the trunk of a hickory upside down searching for larvae. A squall of rain passed over. Raindrops ran down the silken stems of the grass on the path. The sharp notes of a phoebe sounded in the deepening gloom. Well lost to where I came from, my senses were spellbound with the walking, with the hush and quiet, with this particular place and its spirit. My head a bit giddy, I could feel my heart beating beneath my shirt. There were nameless feelings riding the winds, and even intimations of menace, foreboding, warning. This was a lonely, seldom-visited place. I could turn up one of the arcades opening off the hollow and work my way up the forested passageway, up into the shadowed shut-ins that sheltered fern-bordered pools, turn a narrow corner made of mossy boulders and stumble onto . . . what? A sight, a spectacle, a discovery, a glimpse of something lost, a marvel, a theophany – or nothing much! But anything could happen.

I stooped down next to a deep pool in the creek. In the mud nearby were the crisscrossed tracks of deer and wild turkey. As I gulped water from my cupped hands, I could feel that the clear pool tapped all the way down to the fierce core of the Ozarks where subterranean rivers rush and roar in darkness. A neighbor had told me once that the ancient Osage peoples who lived here long ago had sometimes navigated their canoes through these underground rivers. The sweet gums, ash, white oaks, and hickories that stood on the creek banks all leaned in over the pool. Their leaves trembled in the slight breeze. The still waters reflected a small patch of sky above the encircling trees, and in the mirrored reflection I could see also the rocky palisaded heights and high stone eyries beneath the ridges, which echoed the far-off cry of a red-tailed hawk cruising beneath the clouds.

Just about the time you have lost your faith in the world, something comes along to restore it. My thirst slaked, I climbed up to a rock ledge above sheltering flowering columbines and sat quietly in the gloom. I had crossed some kind of threshold here. New and unconsidered aspects dawned in me. Impossible dreams awakened. I became convinced that I had been sleepwalking most of my life. "The wildest and most desolate scenes," wrote Thoreau, "are strangely familiar to me." This rocky bend in the hollow where

I rested was a sacred place – as holy as any church sanctuary.

"Behold," exclaimed King Solomon after completing his temple thousands of years ago, "the heaven and the heaven of heavens cannot contain thee: how much less this house that I have builded?" Lying on that rock ledge above the drinking pool I found the lichen-decorated stone that I pocketed to take home. That stone on my shelf was a lodestone, ever pointing to a great mystery that is everywhere. It spoke to me of the need to keep my image of God footloose and large and fancy-free. The Creator is wholly other, yet in all things. Nature reminds us again and again of this. Poet and farmer Wendell Berry points out the crucial importance of keeping this always in mind.

> Solomon and St. Paul insisted on the largeness and at-largeness of God, setting God free, so to speak, from ideas about him. He is not to be fenced in, under human control, like some domestic creature; *he is the wildest being in existence.* The presence of his spirit in us is our wildness, our oneness with the wildness of Creation. That is why subduing the things of nature is so dangerous, and why it so often results in evil, in separation and desecration. It is why the poets of our tradition so often have given nature the role, not only of mother or grandmother, but of the highest earthly teacher and judge, a figure of great mystery and power.

Nature can be the antidote to idolatry, keeping us from clutching those tight definitions of the Great Mystery that screen from our view the sacredness of the world and that can drain us of the rushing blood of hope like some pale vampire. My shelf-stone became a smoldering coal that kindled tongues of fire for a pentecost full of the bright winds God walks down every single day.

A Long and Loving Look

Still the haunted stone on my shelf was not done with me. Because it had me caught in a trap. Though wonderfully decorated with those telltale glittery snail-trails of God, after a time it made me crestfallen and sad to glimpse it perched up there. We searchers and nature lovers always begin with beauty and grace — and rightfully so. But before long, if we are honest with ourselves, this question comes and gives us pause: if beauty and grace are such wise and powerful wizards, then why is their potent sorcery not enough to conjure away ugliness and ease or hold back the recurring pain, loneliness, and suffering of life? Through our strange genetics we humans are the walking wounded, the animals that cry, and beauty can dry the tears only for a while.

The only way out of this trap, for me, was to discover a new way of looking at things, a perspective that was made equally of acceptance, humility, and praise. Anything less was counterfeit. And necessity demanded not only a way of looking, a point of view, but also a workable and practical exercise that would give this point of view legs on which to stand. The stone turned out to be a stepping stone ... to prayer.

The haunting beckoned me toward a new enlarged kind of praying — a contemplative strain that was profoundly engaging because it was a wholeheartedly honest and genuine response to a very real, very deep need. When we look at the world and can't look away, then we take in the laundry just as it is and fold it away into the right drawers, then we begin to learn that contemplative way of seeing so long honored in our spiritual traditions. Thomas Merton teaching prayer to the novices at Gethsemani Abbey told them: "To pray is to enter into mystery, and when we do not enter into the unknown, we do not pray." One person called contemplative praying "a long loving look at the real." M. Scott Peck, bestselling author and psychiatrist, defined mental health as "a courageous dedication to reality." Contemplative praying is one good way to sustain that dedication and resolve.

Contemplative prayer, I found, is one of the best ways to derive benefit from nature's wildness and to reverence her beauty and celebrate her blessings. Prayer with nature has always been a rich source of nourishment in the spiritual life. We drink deeply from the wells of her vigor, slaking a thirst that can never be completely quenched. We never get done with it. Prayer with nature is a passionate listening to the beating heart of the world. It is looking at things as they are. And it is always praise. During walks in the woods, hikes in the mountains, strolls along the shoreline, we share in a bountiful common heritage. We take lasting delight in the way the winds stir the aspen leaves in a Colorado canyon, or the way the moonlight gleams on snowy ridgelines high in the Montana wilderness. The flowering dogwoods on pastel hillsides in Appalachia, the lowering sun shrouded and wreathed in fog off the California coast, the fiesta of color and riotous shape in Utah's canyonlands, the New England autumn, the Grand Canyon's north rim at sunrise. Another litany begins, world without end.

Certainly nowadays when we spend time with nature we confront the desperate need for redemption and conversion of our way of life. Environmentalists daily fight the battle to keep America's last scrap of wilderness out of the hands of corporate greed, to protect our air and our water. Hour by hour the forests topple, the deserts expand, the topsoil slips away. The whales are slaughtered. Part of the ozone layer disappears. Our earth's life is being destroyed.

The stone sitting on my shelf reminds me of this as well. The thought of all this bounty and beauty passing away brings an ache that is well-nigh unbearable. The delighted sparkle of winter sunlight on water dulled. The magic flute of the wood thrush on a summer afternoon silenced. The soaring, sharp-eyed eagles gunned down forever. Nature's vulnerability, her fragility gives me pause, frightens me. I am afraid to risk my love with the bulldozers close by. What kinds of pain could equal the hopeless shipwrecked

desolation of an April sunrise without its bird ser-
enade or an October woodland stripped leafless of
its oaks and elms and hickories slapdashed with
colors?

A wise man wrote long ago some wonderful
words: "It is beauty that will save the world!" I think I
believe that. But what did he mean? It is almost a plat-
itude nowadays that the future of the planet depends
on our ability to reawaken a sense of the sacred, of
the holy. What are the real connections here? How
does this work? Can a bloodshot Arizona sunset re-
verse the troublesome outcomes of our shortsighted
public policy? Can an afternoon encounter in a mountain meadow knee-deep in shooting star and Indian
paintbrush blow the whistle finally on our greed and
consumer avarice? Can a tiny indigo bunting chirping
from a treetop bring gentleness and understanding to
racism's stiff necks and hearts or soften the rage of
nations at one another?

Maybe the whole thing works something like this.

A long and loving look at the natural world we
inhabit can actually change us. We can become different persons. In his book *The Universe Is a Green
Dragon*, physicist Brian Swimme points out that
when you stand in the presence of the moon, for
example, you become a new creation. There is an ac-
tual physical interaction between the photons from
the moon and the optical nerve cells in your brain.
The feeling of awe that arises in the presence of the
dazzling and luminous night sky is as much the creation of the moon and stars as it is yours. The universe

conspires with us in that moment of contemplation. It enters into us in a new way. We become something other than what we were before. "To live," Swimme writes, "is to enter this beauty, surrounded by enchantment, summoned by magnificence."

So, captivated, charmed, and entranced by the world, an inner and outer evolution takes place. While surprised once again by spring's bursting wildflowers out in the bright morning fields or while stalking the rare orchids of praise in green summer forests, I begin to notice that I too, in my own way, am beginning to bloom and to flourish.

Praying with nature is not just a good way to spend some idle moments. An hour of ardent birdwatching is an hour of letting go of myself as the center of things. Anyone who can be content to perch on a rock for an hour and listen to the southwestern desert come alive at sunset or watch the nighthawks rise and plummet on carefree currents of air over the Kansas prairie, anyone who is busy awakening and nourishing that appreciation of the wholeness in nature is also developing an ability to live more fully, more heartily, more effectively, more genuinely. Enjoyment and contemplative attention put me in touch with my own best energies. My capacity to grapple creatively with life's most difficult challenges is increased.

I know that somehow I am a better person for this lifelong love affair with the natural world. Awakened to a passionate reverence I want, with all my heart, to be a person who is great of soul. This life of contemplation enlarges the very core of my soul. There is more room for compassion within me.

Sharing Heartbeats

The abundant payoff in learning to love the earth is a constant theme in Native American spirituality. The Navajo people of the American Southwest identify this contemplative stance toward nature by the phrase "walking in beauty." And walking in beauty to them is essential to their lives. Many of their religious ceremonies center around what is called the "Beautyway." This time of prayer and ceremony and creativity is a spiritual invocation, calling on the harmony and order they see in the desert landscape around them in an effort to renew and restore the harmony and order within their own souls.

When I pray with nature I experience myself as part of a whole, one relationship within a vast network of relationships. I share the muffled rhythm of a heartbeat with the toad, the muskrat, the vesper sparrow, and the hawk. I even share life with the lichens. So the misty mountain vistas, the sad far-away call of the mourning dove, the pungent smells of the autumn rain – all the marvels of this beauty way – provoke in me both love and understanding. The mystery of sharing flesh and bone with other life is awakened. Everything that lives is holy! Slowly I begin to change. Temper tantrums yield to a more tender sympathy. Resentments fade. Envy is short-circuited. I begin to consider even the possibility of beginning to forgive others. In my prayer I stumble upon the simple, yet elusive, mechanisms and machineries – hell, factories – of joy.

Nature teaches us compassion. And she brings lessons of hope to the troubled spirit as well. Henry David Thoreau, America's great nature poet, wrote, "Anyone who really listens and hears the rippling of rivers will never utterly despair of anything." Intimacy with nature brings encounters that suggest there is more here than meets the eye. We see resemblances, suggestions, beckonings. Like the Navajo we invoke the beauty outside to foster and protect the beauty inside, but also to remind us of infinite possibilities and promise. The world we live in is a sleeping beauty, dreamed by the wild soul of God, kissed awake by Time. "Occasionally one sees," writes Barry Lopez, "something fleeting in the land, a moment when line, color and movement intensify and something sacred is revealed, leading one to believe that there is another realm of reality corresponding to the physical one but different."

Sometimes I come to the scenic overlook, stand at the rail for a moment, and then wander off. And sometimes I gape and stand amazed at the fiery hearth of a mountain sunset, my shoes soaked by the dew-washed grass. I sit later by the campfire, bedazzled by summer stars. I wonder. I am endlessly puzzled by things. And I know the conclusive answers to my questions are locked away in unreachable trunks in high dark attics and in the halls of our ancient myths and in the high-energy physics labs. But in the end I have harvested some rich and rare delights and unforgettable savorings. I am quite happy to be perched up in the stout branches of mystery, listening to the silences, sniffing the incense of summer breezes. I wouldn't trade places with anyone. And I murmur thanksgivings while the fair moon rejoices in the clear and cloudless night.

I return to nature again and again – because I want to learn to be better than I am.

From outside my window come the sounds of the city, the rumblings and swish of traffic, the noise of ceaseless activity. Leaning back in my chair, I become quiet for a moment and muse on what lies beyond the outskirts of town, far down in Mad Dog Hollow. There, the owls still call with ghostly voices to one another in the midnight hush of the forest. There the soft rains still whisper in the pines. The winds stir, shuffle through the fallen leaves, and then lie calm again. Mists rise off the currents of the river in the mornings. And those Ozark stones haunt me now more than ever.

Recommended Reading

Berry, Thomas, with Thomas Clarke, S.J. *Befriending the Earth: A Theology of Reconciliation between Humans and the Earth*. Mystic, Conn.: Twenty-Third Publications, 1991.

Center for Science in the Public Interest. *Ninety-nine Ways to a Simple Lifestyle*. New York: Anchor Doubleday, 1977.

Elgin, Duane. *Voluntary Simplicity: Toward a Way of Life That Is Outwardly Simple, Inwardly Rich*. New York: William Morrow & Co., 1981.

Ferder, Fran. *Words Made Flesh: Scripture, Psychology and Human Communication*. Notre Dame, Ind.: Ave Maria Press, 1987.

Foster, Richard J. *Freedom of Simplicity*. San Francisco: Harper San Francisco, 1989.

Fox, Matthew. *Creation Spirituality: Liberating Gifts for Peoples of the Earth*. San Francisco: HarperSanFrancisco, 1991.

———. *Original Blessing*. Santa Fe, N.M.: Bear and Company, 1983.

Granberg-Michaelson, Wesley. *A Worldly Spirituality: The Call to Take Care of the Earth.* San Francisco: Harper & Row, 1984.

Hays, Edward. *Secular Sanctity.* Easton, Kans.: Forest of Peace Books, 1984.

Livingston, Patricia H. *Lessons of the Heart: Celebrating the Rhythms of Life.* Notre Dame, Ind.: Ave Maria Press, 1992.

Lovelock, James E. *Gaia: A New Look at Life on Earth.* New York: Oxford University Press, 1979.

Longacre, Doris Janzen. *Living More with Less.* Scottdale, Pa.: Herald Press, 1980.

May, Gerald. *The Awakened Heart: Living beyond Addiction.* San Francisco: Harper San Francisco, 1991.

Montgomery, Dan. *How to Survive Practically Anything.* Ann Arbor, Mich.: Servant Publications, 1993.

Pelphry, Brant. *Christ Our Mother: Julian of Norwich.* Way of the Christian Mystics 7. Wilmington, Del.: Michael Glazier, 1989.

Rifkin, Jeremy, ed. *The Green Lifestyle Handbook: 1001 Ways You Can Heal the Earth.* New York: Henry Holt and Co., 1990.

Rohr, Richard. *Simplicity: The Art of Living.* New York: Crossroad, 1991.

Roszak, Theodore. *The Voice of the Earth.* New York: Simon and Schuster, 1993.

Sale, Kirkpatrick. *Dwellers in the Land: The Bioregional Vision.* San Francisco: Sierra Club Books, 1985.

Shi, David. *The Simple Life: Plain Living and High Thinking in American Culture.* New York: Oxford University Press, 1985.

Shi, David, ed. *In Search of the Simple Life: American Voices Past and Present.* Layton, Utah: Peregrine Smith, 1986.

Sinetar, Marsha. *Ordinary People as Monks and Mystics.* Mahwah, N.J.: Paulist Press, 1986.

———. *A Way without Words: A Guide for Spiritually Emerging Adults.* Mahwah, N.J.: Paulist Press, 1992.

Woods, Richard. *Christian Spirituality: God's Presence through the Ages.* Chicago: Thomas More Press, 1989.